D1553776

RABBIT DECOLONIZES THE FOREST

Stories from the Euchee Reservation

Rabbit decolonizes the forest. Illustration by Adam Youngbear.

RABBIT DECOLONIZES THE FOREST

Stories from the Euchee Reservation

Gregory H. Bigler

Foreword by Kristen A. Carpenter

UNIVERSITY OF OKLAHOMA PRESS : NORMAN

This book is published with the generous assistance of the Kerr Foundation, Inc.

Library of Congress Cataloging-in-Publication Data

Names: Bigler, Gregory H., author. | Carpenter, Kristen A., foreworder.
Title: Rabbit decolonizes the forest : stories from the Euchee Reservation / Gregory H. Bigler.
Other titles: Stories from the Euchee Reservation
Description: Norman : University of Oklahoma Press, [2024] | Contents: Growing Up Euchee; The Longest Walk, July 1978; Just Leave It Till Morning; Wild Onion Dinners; Bill and I Go to the Supreme Court; Seven Thousand Dzogala; Rabbit and Turkeys; Jackson and the Old Man; Jackson's Little Friend; Decolonizing the Spirit World; Shajwane and Gojithlah (Rabbit and Monster); Rabbit Decolonizes the Forest; The United League of Rabbits; Visiting Uncle John; Euchee Doctors; Jackson Almost Learned to Doctor; Wilson Gets a Wife, Almost; You Need to Get Out of Here; Shaggy—Indians Don't Get Lost; Billy and the Indoor Dance; Billy Plans to Doctor Dzehne; Soup Dance and Chief; Chief Comingdeer's Nephew; After the Dance— Whose Kid Is This?; Fixing Medicine for Funerals; Dzoti Dodi; The Journey; How Rabbit Gets His Short Tail; Crane Visits Buffalo; Wolf Eats Tofu for Lunch; Pray for Us; Winter Solstice—A Modern Di'ile; Shajwane Gets Served; Little Man Makes a Jailbreak; Jackson's Friend Takes a Road Trip; Jackson Speaks for His Niece; The Euchee Parting; Rabbit and the Last Old Woman | Summary: "A collection of short stories mixing traditional and newly created di'ile (Euchee stories involving animals), personal recollections, and short fiction"—Provided by publisher.
Identifiers: LCCN 2023037128 | ISBN 978-0-8061-9363-2 (paperback)
Subjects: LCSH: Yuchi Indians—Oklahoma—Folklore. | Animals—Folklore. | Tales—Oklahoma. | Oklahoma—Social life and customs. | LCGFT: Folk tales.
Classification: LCC E99.Y9 B54 2024 | DDC 398.2089979—dc23/ eng/20230824
LC record available at https://lccn.loc.gov/2023037128

The paper in this book meets the guidelines for permanence and durability of the Committee on Production Guidelines for Book Longevity of the Council on Library Resources, Inc. ∞

Copyright © 2024 by Gregory H. Bigler. Published by the University of Oklahoma Press, Norman, Publishing Division of the University. Manufactured in the U.S.A.

All rights reserved. No part of this publication may be reproduced, stored in a retrieval system, or transmitted, in any form or by any means, electronic, mechanical, photocopying, recording, or otherwise—except as permitted under Section 107 or 108 of the United States Copyright Act—without the prior written permission of the University of Oklahoma Press. To request permission to reproduce selections from this book, write to Permissions, University of Oklahoma Press, 2800 Venture Drive, Norman OK 73069, or email rights.oupress@ou.edu.

To Josephine Wildcat Bigler
(May 24, 1921–June 4, 2016)

Contents

Part 3. Indian Doctors and Dances

Part 4. Shajwane and Friends

Part 5. Final Matters

Foreword

by Kristen A. Carpenter

I first read *Rabbit Decolonizes the Forest: Stories from the Euchee Reservation* on a plane. I read it cover to cover, nearly without stopping. When I reached the end, put the manuscript down on the tray table, and looked up at the passengers around me, it was like emerging from a dream. A dream of thick Oklahoma nights, men's voices singing ancient prayers, women shaking shells, and crickets keeping up the chorus audible during the breaks between dances. A dream in which animals and humans can still understand one another and Spirits come to visit over a cup of coffee.

Life at Oklahoma ceremonial grounds is a dream of pure joy, palpable during particular moments when the leader calls for the turtles or the fire swirls into purple just before sending bright sparks into the darkness. Or maybe, for those staying up all night, the moment of joy comes when they make it past the 3:00 or 4:00 A.M. hour and somehow, despite physical and emotional fatigue, find the strength to keep going. As Judge Bigler says, "It's hard to be Indian."

Of course, Judge Bigler's stories are not a dream at all. Judge Bigler writes as a Euchee tribal citizen and a member of Polecat Ceremonial Grounds. He is a parent and grandparent, a Harvard Law School graduate, and a longtime district court judge at the Muscogee (Creek) Nation. He has co-counseled Indian law cases before the U.S. Supreme Court, mentored generations of Indian law attorneys, published law review articles, and without a doubt run more marathons than any other Indian lawyer. As my teenagers would say, these stories take place "IRL," or "in real life."

In real life, as Judge Bigler's stories make clear, Indian people are keeping their traditions alive, listening to their chiefs, speaking Indigenous languages, and navigating contemporary circumstances, whether it's kids (and grown-ups) sending gossipy texts at the stomp grounds, wolf eating tofu in the forest, or traditional Euchee teasing loquacious academics about their decolonizing methodologies. The charming Shajwane, Mr. Rabbit, remains popular even after many years on the Indian story circuit. In a new development, we've heard Rabbit is wearing a fancy down vest and bolo tie over at Shawnee.

This is a world that I am able to visit from time to time through friends and relations at ceremonial grounds. I cherish these times but also understand that it's not nearly the same for me, as an occasional visitor, as it is for the people—whether Cherokees, Muscogees, Shawnees, Seminoles, or Euchee—who keep the fire, the towns, the ballgames, and dances alive day in and day out. They take on the tremendous work of cleaning the grounds, repairing arbors, cutting wood, preparing food, taking medicine, dancing and singing and praying all night long, sometimes in the rain, to carry out the ways of their people. These are cultural traditions handed down from generation to generation, suppressed for hundreds of years by governments and churches, still surviving today. In some Indian communities, the old ways are just barely surviving when, of thousands of enrolled tribal citizens, maybe only a few hundred are traditional practitioners.

The U.S. Supreme Court has recently vindicated what members of ceremonial grounds have known all along. The places in Oklahoma where Indian people live, pray, and dance are Indian lands. In the 2020 case of *Jimcy McGirt v. State of Oklahoma,* the Court ruled that the Muscogee (Creek) Nation remains "Indian Country" for purposes of federal criminal jurisdiction pursuant to several treaties dating to 1832 when the federal government decided to move the Muscogees (and Euchee) from their traditional lands in the East to a federal territory in the West. Thousands and thousands of Indians lost their lives during this Trail of Tears, but the survivors had the treaties' guarantees of a new homeland to keep them going. The *McGirt* decision, based on a very plain reading of these treaties, is surely correct, and it means that the Muscogee (Creek) Nation government has jurisdiction over a significant portion of northeastern Oklahoma. Ditto for the Cherokees, Choctaws, Chickasaws, and Seminoles, who all have very similar treaties.

What law now applies in the Muscogee (Creek) Nation—a territory comprising a good portion of Oklahoma? To some extent federal and state laws still apply. But, most importantly, the laws of the tribes themselves apply to many aspects of life in Indian Country. Thus *McGirt* marks an opportunity for the renewal and resurgence of tribal law, an important phenomenon that corresponds with the global human rights movement.

The *United Nations Declaration on the Rights of Indigenous Peoples* was adopted by the UN General Assembly in 2007 and supported by the United States in 2010. This document was drafted in large part by Indigenous Peoples themselves, an important culmination of efforts first started by traditional Indian leaders, including Philip Deer of the Muscogee (Creek) Nation and Nuyaka Ground, who traveled to the United Nations in the 1970s to assert their rights. Negotiated over several decades, the *Declaration* recognizes Indigenous Peoples' rights to self-determination, equality, religion, language, and culture. And for many people, it represents a new day in advocacy for Indigenous Peoples as a matter of universal rights.

Importantly, the *Declaration* recognizes the right of tribes to exist as distinct peoples with their own "laws, customs, and traditions." It recognizes Indigenous Peoples' rights to maintain their religious sites, Indigenous languages, sacred plants, traditional medicines—or, as Muscogee people might put it, the *Declaration* recognizes the rights of Indigenous Peoples to maintain their "ways." The laws, customs, and traditions of the Muscogee (Creek) Nation (MCN) include the tribe's constitution and its legislative code, the rulings of the district court and MCN Supreme Court, and the *Declaration* itself. In 2016, the Muscogee (Creek) Nation (under the tutelage of Judge Bigler) translated the *United Nations Declaration* into the Muscogee language and adopted the Muscogee version (*MDRIP*) into tribal law. The *MDRIP* recognizes that, pursuant to Article 31 of the *Declaration*, "*Hiyomakat pum ayetv pum wihokat vcacvket omet sahkopanetvt okot omes*" or, in English, "Now this is our ways that was given to us and is very sacred and is not to play with."

These ways, which can be understood as the laws, customs, and traditions of the Muscogee and Euchee people, are highly complex, deeply embedded, and totally alive. Members of the stomp grounds abide by them—following the directions of their chiefs, carrying out ceremonial rules handed down generations ago, honoring the Spirit world with offerings and recognition, maintaining peace and order at the grounds, caring for children while teaching them proper ways of behavior, and so on. All of these laws, customs, and traditions, and others, structure society as it appears in *Rabbit Decolonizes the Forest: Stories from the Euchee Reservation*. These laws are challenged by so many things—the history of conquest and colonization, generations of social and economic deprivation, and the temptations of contemporary society—but they remain alive, carried out to this very day when the stomp-ground chief calls someone to come cut the wood, and sure enough he goes, even though it's five o'clock in the morning.

In conclusion, I confess to being an academic whom Judge Bigler has teased for trying to decolonize various things. Guilty as charged and in awe of the power of this book to transport readers to the world of Spirits and coffee, ribbon skirts and relatives, hard times and humorous ones, within Euchee Country.

Introduction

E uchee Country, in Creek County and northern Okmulgee County, just south and west of Tulsa, Oklahoma, doesn't look much like what one thinks of as a reservation. Technically, Euchee Country is within or part of the Muscogee Nation reservation, but we Euchee tend to refer to where we live as the "Euchee rez" or simply the "rez." Most of our Euchee allotments got "sold" off in the 1930s and '40s—or stolen, legally stolen for the most part, but stolen nonetheless. Driving through the area, one sees small towns, several small but increasingly large cities, and the increasingly sprawling Tulsa. So many white and Black people, one must look hard sometimes to even find Indians. Yet, if you get to the right spots, the right places, it remains Euchee Country. Sometimes it comes into existence only for short periods—on the weekends at stomp dance, at Green Corn, during funerals, at Pickett Chapel, even at Walmart when we run into one another. Maybe at some parties; I can't vouch for that, though I hear stories.

In saying Euchee Country comes into existence, I mean those moments when Euchee culture and society come into the open from where we hold them hidden inside us as we move within the mainstream society that surrounds us. That flowering happens less and less frequently now. So many of our relationships are contextually non-Euchee. We still maintain our Euchee family, church, and ceremonial relations, but so many other interactions and institutions are non-Euchee or non-Native. Not surprising, considering we draw so much upon non-Native

Grandma Lizzie (Bighead) Wildcat
and Mom (Josephine Wildcat Bigler), circa 1921.

sources or interactions—schools, work, TV, media and social media—
almost all fundamentally non-Indian, let alone non-Euchee.

In the 1960s, Pickett Chapel used to conduct services in Euchee; now
we are fifty years removed from a Euchee-language preacher. The question is how we can continue to create more of those moments of Indian
Country. Fortunately, we still have our Euchee hymns, and once again
we can hear Euchee prayers, thanks to a Euchee-language revival. But
Pickett Chapel is as often filled with non-Euchee as with Euchee wor-
shipers. Through a constant washing over us of this mainstream society, a dilution easily, unconsciously occurs of our own unique tribal
identity, a subjugation of our Eucheeness. Though unintentional at this
point, this gradual erosion is perhaps more effective than, or perhaps
the end result of, the forced boarding schools of the 1920s and '30s that
cut Indian boys' hair, suppressed Native languages, and attacked
tribal religion.[1] These remaining modern moments of Euchee interactions become metaphysical reservations of Euchee life within the
physical boundaries of the Muscogee Reservation, which was re-
recognized in 2020 in the United States Supreme Court decision *McGirt
v. Oklahoma.*

"Indian Country" is a federal Indian law term, defined in the *United
States Code,* Title 18. It refers to a place set aside for the use of Indians
as Indians. That legal term works well here to express a place, time,
culture, or people that maintain Indianness, or, as in the stories that
follow, remains Euchee. We want our Euchee life to breathe. This is all
the more difficult for us Euchee for being within the Muscogee Nation.
We closely share a culture with them, though there are distinct differences that culturally conversant Euchee and Muscogee recognize. The
most distinct difference is that our Euchee language is an isolate, that
is, unrelated to any other language. One is required to go back some
six thousand years to find connections of Euchee to any other language.
Thus, Euchee have been Euchee since before Rome, before the ancient
Greeks, before the Egyptians built the pyramids, before the ancient
Shang dynasty of China. As our ceremonies proclaim, we are still here.
At least for now.

My mother, who passed away in 2016, was born in 1921, the oldest
of her mom and dad's five children. A full-blood Euchee, she and her
four siblings grew up in the Sapulpa area, speaking Euchee, going to
Pickett Chapel, where services were conducted in the Euchee language.
They began living with their grandmother when my mother was about
ten or twelve. Her *golaha* (grandmother) made them follow traditional

restrictions and medicine practices, even as they attended Christian church.

A few years before she passed away, we began taking my mother to Duck Creek's Ribbon Dance. Polecat is the main Euchee stomp ground, the one we brought with us from Georgia in the 1830s. We are all Euchee, though, so we try to help the other two Euchee grounds, Duck Creek and Iron Post, when they have their dances. Duck Creek's Green Corn usually occurs the last weekend in June, about two or three weeks before ours at Polecat. The Ducks hold their Ribbon Dance on Friday night before Saturday Green Corn, whereas we at Polecat hold ours on Green Corn Day. Duck's Ribbon Dance usually has a lot of visitors that come to watch, not just other Euchee but also Creeks, Cherokees, and Shawnees from those ceremonial grounds, who share the stomp-dance culture. In addition, there are many other non-Euchee Indians and non-Indians, who do not stomp dance but are friends and just want to look on. This, though, is not a pow-wow; it is religious, it is sacred, something given to us by Gohahtine (the Creator) and the medicines very long ago, long before the white man arrived on our shores. But we enjoy sharing it with our friends and family, in a respectful way. We just don't want to advertise it.

It is late afternoon, sometime after 6:00 P.M., maybe closer to 7:00 P.M., when they start the Ribbon Dance. The sixty or seventy old women, young women, and little girls who participate are all dressed in their traditional ribbon dresses or skirts, with the namesake long ribbons flowing from their hair, their turtle shells or cans tied around their legs. Each of the items they wear—skirts, ribbons, aprons, Indian paint on their faces—likely has an explanation, sometimes a long story for why they are used. We explain our dances through stories about White Crane, giant lizards, the Sun, tobacco, medicines, Scottish traders, Spirits, and Old People now gone. Some stories we tell among ourselves; many stories have probably been forgotten in our many upheavals, removals, and losses of elders.

It is still hot at 7:00 P.M., especially in the full sun of late June in Oklahoma. Many of the women spent the day cooking in the dozen or so camps that make up Duck Creek Grounds. As the Ribbon Dancers are led out of their camps to the square ground with its three brush arbors, many of the camps continue getting ready for the evening meal they will serve the dancers and visitors after the Ribbon Dance and the Old Man Dance, which is done right after the Ribbon Dance. Those two dances finish sometime around dusk, around 9:00 P.M. There can be up to five hundred or more people sitting there looking on, between home bunch and visitors, with all the cars, trucks, and vehicles parked two or three deep on the grass around the outside of the square grounds. With lawn chairs placed in front of the vehicles, people are waving and visiting each other as they sit and wait.

During the 1920s and '30s, my mother spent time growing up in the Duck Creek area. Her aunt Sakie Bighead lived just a few miles down the road from the stomp grounds, though the current Duck Creek Ground itself was not started until the early 1940s. There had been a Euchee stomp ground in that area before Duck Creek was started, maybe closer to Aunt Sakie's, but my understanding is that it went down (stopped dancing) around the time of allotment in 1906. Although my mom grew up in the church, she knew many of those at the ceremonial grounds; they were her friends and relations. Toward the end of her life, my mom, as one of the oldest full-blood Euchee and a fluent Euchee speaker, was respected and always welcomed.

The last time we took my mother to Duck's Ribbon Dance she must have felt nostalgic, thinking of the times she spent in the area as a young girl. Aunt Sakie's house is on Hectorville Rd., or 221st Rd., the road we take from Highway 75 to the grounds, just south of Tulsa County, in northern Okmulgee County. She talked about riding down there with her mother and father from their place in Sapulpa. I guess that was before her grandmother took in her siblings and her due to her mom and dad's drinking. Aunt Sakie had one daughter, May, who was maybe a couple years younger than my mother. Back then, the area was rural, with numerous Euchee living in the area, their allotments spread over a several-mile radius.

At the time of allotment around 1900, there were approximately eight hundred people listed as members of "Euchee Town" within the Creek Nation. Those population numbers did not likely increase much by the time my mother was growing up. Duck Creek was one of the three or four old Euchee settlements in the Creek Nation, the other being Polecat (around Sapulpa and Kellyville) and the Depew or Gypsy area. Those three or four Euchee settlements were related and residents intermarried one another. However, they had slight dialect, or accent, differences to their speech. Nothing major, maybe ending certain words with a long "a" instead of a long "e" sound. But it was enough for those speakers to know where a Euchee grew up, where their parents were from because of their speech. Now we are just happy if someone speaks Euchee, and probably many young people don't know the differences.

The road to Duck Creek is paved now, but when my mother was young, it was a dirt road. I don't think they bothered to gravel the roads till the 1940s or '50s, and they were not paved until more recently. A mile or two east of Sakie's place is a small country store at Hectorville. I don't think there was anything else there except some Indians, but they called it Hectorville, maybe in hopes that it would become something someday. Calling it a store might be kind, as it was not much more than a small stone shed with things for sale. It used to have a sandstone exterior, though it may now have a different façade. But that little store is still there, and apparently it was there when my mom was growing up in the 1920s and '30s.

My mother said she and May would sometimes walk to the store, maybe to get a pop, maybe just for something to do. She told how one time she and May walked there and then decided they would go on to visit a Euchee woman, Micco Behen's relation, maybe his sister (though I was not clear on that from my mother), who lived a mile or so north of the store. I was told by other old Euchee relations that Micco Behen had been a chief at our grounds, Polecat, in the 1930s but started going to church, and probably gave up his chief's seat by 1936 when we moved Polecat ground a mile west to where it now sits. Micco probably passed away in the 1940s. One of my older relations said that Micco Behen must have become a lay leader at Pickett because during one of those hot July or August Sundays, he was leading the sermon. This was before air-conditioning, when the windows would be open in the faint hope that a breeze might come through, maybe aided by some of those old standing floor fans. Between the stifling, still heat in the small church house and the perhaps too-long sermon, people were falling asleep. Micco saw them nodding off and went in front of the pulpit, stomped his feet, and let out a "Yooo!!" as if starting a stomp dance song. Everyone snapped their eyes open, looking at Micco Behen. He was laughing as he went back behind the pulpit and started preaching again. Back then, Euchee churchgoers did not go to stomp dance, though some of them were stomp dancers before converting to Christianity. When Micco started that stomp dance song, it startled everyone, confusing some, maybe scaring some who thought stomp dance was evil even if they followed other traditional practices.

I don't know much about Micco Behen's sister, except my mother said she had no children of her own, so she was happy to see two young Euchee girls walking up the road to visit. My mother said she and May spent most of the day playing, visiting in Euchee, and helping her.

Finally, as it was getting late in the afternoon, the woman told the girls they'd better be getting back to May's home. So they left and walked the few miles back to Aunt Sakie's. I asked my mother how old the woman was, thinking she was probably in her thirties. My mom thought about it and answered, "Oh, she must have probably been in her sixties or seventies." I laughed, thinking of two little girls deciding on their own to go visit, spending all day helping and playing with an elderly Euchee woman.

This short story of taking my mother to Duck Creek covers so much: how two little Euchee girls walked to an older Euchee woman's house to spend the day, highlighting how our people used to easily, naturally bathe in the Euchee language, culture, and relationships, letting them wash over us. How memories, short stories, animals, and Spirits all combine to make us Euchee. In today's world, in doing Euchee things we must know why we do them, what it is that we want as a result. As the former head judge at the Muscogee (Creek) Nation district court for some ten years, I initiated a project in 2015 to translate the *United Nations Declaration on the Rights of Indigenous Peoples* into the Muscogee language. To do this, we needed, and were fortunate to have, several fluent Muscogee speakers and several Muscogee ceremonial grounds *mekvlke* (plural of *meko*, or "chiefs")—who of course were fluent Muscogee speakers—participate in the project. Working our way through the *Declaration*, we came to Article 31, which discusses our right to our cultural heritage, knowledge, traditions, medicines, and literature, and our right to control them.[2]

The speakers had a literal translation of Article 31, but they began discussing the article in detail, what it meant, what its purpose was. They remembered how the old men at their ceremonial grounds, different but similar to our Euchee grounds, talked about these very things in their Muscogee language. What they said this meant, in their language, when literally translated back into English was: "Now this is our ways that was given to us and is very sacred and is not to play with."[3]

When I used to do a lot of federal litigation, especially appellate work, my now deceased partner Bill Rice used to say, "Tell the court *why* we should win, they can figure out *how* we win." We always presented the law and arguments, but it was important to understand why it mattered. If we want to preserve our ways of life, the sacred, the social, the daily mundane Euchee-infused ways, we must remember those people who tie those places to us and to this world. When those connections such as my mother had to Aunt Sakie, to old lady Behen, or to those old

Euchee settlements finally disappear, then those things they tied to this world also disappear. The why for us are those places and stories, those interactions that used to naturally occur, such as between my mother, cousin May, and old lady Behen.

These ways are sacred, and we have obligations to them. They are waiting for us. When the outside world or world around us overruns them, our fires go out, the medicines disappear, and those Euchee places are no more. But this way of understanding has no legal foundation, no protections in Western thought. Through the telling, we keep life in our places and our ways. And now, we perhaps have an outside ally in these efforts in the *United Nations Declaration*. Stories explain why we are important, how places and small memories about little Euchee girls keep us alive.

The stories that follow mix personal recollections; traditional Euchee stories (called *di'ile*) usually involving animals, told mostly to children but sometimes between adults; new stories patterned on traditional *di'ile*; and short fiction. They have in common a foundation built on the feeling of Euchee life, a life often woven through with a spiritual nature. Not spiritual in the Western-understood sense of an internal quest for peace or centeredness, but spiritual as in a world filled with animate life, Spirits that interact with us, some Spirits we see or seek, some we feel, some that simply are. We as modern people may not regularly mingle with Spirits, but the traditional Euchee life that still infuses us strongly pulls on that existence. These themes remain a part of us and our Euchee ways as we continue as a people.

In our Euchee world, we hear stories of animal, human, and Spirit adventures in our *di'ile*, but also in the stories explaining our ceremonies and understanding our everyday life—the flitting shadow, the occasional animal messenger, the dreams. In seeing and hearing of these things, one might wonder what happens to these Spirits as they, too, move in the modern Western world, surrounded by housing additions, their descendants and Indian relations long removed, businesses overrunning our Indian places. What happens to them when no one remembers, does not recognize, or no longer believes in those Spirits? Like the old reservation Indians confined to areas bounded by non-Indian territory with no avenue for escape. Our tribal, Indigenous Spirits suffer the same fate as the water sprites of Greek myths, the German fairies, elves, Norse giants, and others that traversed the spiritual world, now no more than stories to fill literary footnotes or billion-dollar screenplays. Ancient lands and ancient sacred sites with beings that no longer have a people to believe in them or tell their stories, their physical places developed out of the spiritual world. Our Spirits are locked in museums, or we see their sacred core taken for New Age purposes, desecrated, and destroyed—the colonization of the spiritual world.

Our people didn't call it magic. It simply was. In English, we call it "our ways," spiritual—that world of Spirits that we are not constantly privy to but which we dwell in. Our traditional people see us moving through both the physical and the spiritual world. Most of us no longer easily live within the spiritual world till we tire in the physical—such as at our ceremonial dances late in the night, in that special hour just before the first faint light of morning arrives. The Old People tried to tell us that when the body is weak, the spirit is strong. Now we wonder if it is too late.

We were filled with those stories when visiting our old aunts and uncles, listening to the old men and woman. Stories of Old People, animals, little balls of light, *gonuh-s'i* (the little people), and others. Sometimes, though, their stories were just stories, sometimes funny; sometimes people going about their life, taking care of family, seeing friends; sometimes of places remembered. Sometimes one was not sure if the old story had actually happened, though it often expressed a truth. All these stories are begging for us to tell them.

Just as those of us who are blessed to still wander through our Euchee life, the stories here wander between recollection, such as from my mother's or elder women's sewing classes, traditional tales called *di'ile*, new stories in the form of traditional *di'ile*, and modern short fiction such as the ones involving Jackson and his friends. All work to imbue a sense, a feel, for the life we still live in, the world around us that we work to tie to our old ways. Sometimes that is done with memories, sometimes it is done by poking fun at ourselves through Shajwane (Rabbit). Whether these stories are true, they all in a sense happened.

This is not a historical narrative or an attempt to educate, but perhaps to better understand the stories one needs some context about the Euchee. We are a small, little-known tribe within the Muscogee (Creek) Nation. We are not, however, Muscogee, nor are we separately federally recognized. We were removed from Georgia on the Trail of Tears in the 1830s with the Muscogee. Our last tribal town, what was called Euchee Town, was located near what is now Columbus, Georgia, located within what is now Fort Benning. We still strongly maintain our traditional religion, which is similar but not identical to the Muscogee's and that of other stomp dance people, who were originally of the southeastern United States. As mentioned, our language is unrelated to any other, and we were down to a handful of elderly Euchee speakers just a few years ago. However, we have seen a significant revival of the language, with young people learning it to fluency. In some ways, we are better off than many larger, better-known tribes, as we are producing new speakers. In that vein, I use some Euchee words in these stories, using the orthography that my mother taught when we began our language classes back in 1990. More recently, the Euchee classes that started after our classes have adopted a different orthography or alphabet to write out Euchee. Like so many other things about us Euchee, nothing is clear. We ourselves write our name in various ways; I use "Euchee" here, but we have also utilized "Yuchi" or even in the past "Uchee." Some also refer to themselves as Tsoyaha, "Children of the Sun," from the story of how the Sun is the mother of the Euchee.[4] Regardless, the orthography used here is perhaps a bit more readable for outsiders, so I utilize it throughout. But it is important to note that it is not how one will usually see Euchee written out. I should also point out that the new orthography has at least once been usurped by people claiming falsely to be Euchee in order to try and pretend to be us. We were, and apparently remain, a stubborn people, keeping our ceremonies, language, and community alive and often to ourselves. However, nothing happens by accident, and we rely on just a few people to keep this way alive in our small part of the world to the west and south of Tulsa, Oklahoma.

Hopefully, the following stories convey in some fleeting manner how this way of life feels, a way of life often hidden from view, or at least unnoticed by those around us. Just in the way that my mother and other elders would tell them, no story takes a straight path. They go back, then forward, then perhaps meander sideways. But when done, one realizes, maybe long afterward, "Oh, that is what they were talking about."

Part 1

MEMOIRS

Growing Up Euchee

I begin, as do all stories of Native people, with two stories, gifts from my mother that place her as Euchee in land and time. My mother was born May 24, 1921, and passed away June 4, 2016. My mother was many things, a full-blood Euchee, a preacher's wife, a mother of three boys. She and her family, growing up, spoke only Euchee, centered in Euchee life, albeit Christian. In the 1970s, after we had moved to Milwaukee in the late 1960s, she became active in Indian affairs. She wrote the first of the two narratives in 2013 for a presentation I asked her to make at our Muscogee (Creek) Nation District Court continuing legal education to compare her growing up Euchee during the 1920s and '30s with what occurred during the 1970s prior to the enactment of the Indian Child Welfare Act (ICWA) and with the ICWA status today.

After her death in 2016, we found a journal she kept from her time on the Longest Walk. These excerpts are from her journal. The Longest Walk was organized by the American Indian Movement to draw attention to eleven pieces of legislation then before Congress. It started in February 1978 at Alcatraz Island, California, and ended at the National Mall in Washington, D.C. These excerpts are taken verbatim from that journal.

Josephine (Wildcat) Bigler, senior picture, Southeastern State College
(now Southeastern Oklahoma University), circa 1945.

In the early 1930s, there were five of us children, three boys and
two girls. Our parents were full-blood Euchee who had attended
the Euchee Mission. Mother only completed the third or fourth
grade. Our dad completed the eighth grade.

I lived with my maternal grandmother in my first year of school.
This was the Mounds area. My parents lived in Sapulpa, but they didn't
want me to walk the long distance to Sapulpa school. Both of my grandmothers spoke only Euchee.

Prior to Christianity, they had always followed the traditional
grounds ceremonies. Once the grandmothers accepted Christianity,
they never returned to the grounds. They were very loyal to the church
and continued to observe other traditions of the Euchee tribe. The
paternal grandmother was also a medicine woman. I never knew either
grandfather, as they had died before I was born. Grandfather Wildcat
must have died between 1901 and 1904. Our father was a young boy
when his father died.

In the later '20s and '30s, some of the young relatives had begun to drink. They came to our house to drink. Both parents started drinking. That eventually led to the family breakup. After I had finished the seventh grade in Sapulpa, Father told me we children were going to go live with our grandmother Eliza (Fah-Go-Gweny).

Grandmother Eliza lived six or seven miles south of Sapulpa. There were two houses. One was to sleep in, and the other was to cook in and to eat in. It became too small for ten people. The men eventually built an addition, which was a larger kitchen and dining area, to the house we slept in.

There were no modern conveniences. All we children learned various tasks that were daily.

Grandmother had fields of corn and cotton, two large gardens, an apple orchard, a grape vineyard, peanuts, and a number of pecan trees. There were chickens, hogs, and horses.

In the wintertime, there was time in the evening for sharing and listening to stories told by the elders. Grandmother was a beautiful storyteller.

We children sat on the floor while Grandmother told us Rabbit stories. He was a mischievous animal. Uncle Josie told us about older Euchee banding [together] and helping the Creek Indians fight invaders. Sometimes Euchee who helped others never returned.

We all knew that by Thursday or Friday, we began to think of preparing for a church weekend. Clothes and food had to be prepared and hand carried a mile through the woods.

In later years, three brothers joined the military, and all are deceased. Only Sister and I today are known as elders and help teach and share our Euchee traditions with children and young people.

The Longest Walk, July 1978

Left Milwaukee on Friday, July 7, 1978, with Eva Olsen and Barbara Hill. The day was warm, and we traveled until midnight when we finally found the last available room at a motel (21.00 [dollars]), [in] Irwin, Pennsylvania. Slept late—started about 11:00 A.M., the mountains were beautiful—encountered rain off and on in Alleghenies. Drove into Baltimore about 4:00 P.M. Stopped at 2300 Edmondson to call Barbara Lowery. Fireman at fire station was very solicitous in our behalf. We were in the Black Community and were invited to come into the firehouse while we waited for Barbara Lowery. The fellows offered coffee and—if they should be called out—we must go to the back of the station and remain.

Barbara L. arrived—directed us to Trinitarian House. Discovered Longest Walk Camp located at York, Pa. (40 miles). Backtracked to York, where we found the camp in [the] midst of [a] rally for community. Many, many tribes in old & new vans, pickups, school buses, all makes of cars—in all manner & variety of tents & tipis. Largely traditional people.

Yellow saffron-robed Japanese (Buddhist) have marched, and since joining—walk all the way. Very strong, disciplined people. They are up and at meditation [at] 5:30 A.M. & in the evening. Representatives from Sweden, Spain, and France.

Food distribution (contributed by individuals, groups, churches) is from a U-Haul truck. March staples—fresh fruits, vegetables. Also used clothing—but not much which is actually usable for Longest Walk people. Walking shoes, sox & denims are greatest needs.

Monday—July 10

Prayers offered at each start of walk.

Walk into Baltimore from harbor for rally. Very warm for walking! Walked past historic Lindy Lane Methodist Church (1772), site of historic 1789 Christmas Conference. Very few non-Indian participants at the rally. Bused back to camp site.

Very good response from Black neighborhoods as we ride through their areas. Vernon Bellecourt says the greatest amount of response to camp needs came from Blacks. They understand, in very deep sense, other people's oppression.

Friday—July 14, 1978

Very grateful to Eva and Barbara for going ahead to set up tent today.

Great Day! We break camp early—up at 5:30 A.M.—tent down & packed by 6:30 A.M. Next-to-last leg of journey to Wash., D.C. We eat a hearty breakfast, for we have a long walk today.

Eva and I start together—but I am called out to walk with the elders— great honor to walk with them behind the pipe carriers. Elder from Navaho Nation offers prayer before journey. A number of elders from Lakota and 6 Nations join today. The women are straight and strong—very persistent. Our pace is slower because we have elders today. But the Great Spirit watches over his people and sends a cloud cover to make our walk more endurable. I walk the entire journey—twenty-two miles—and have the blister on each foot to prove it. I never walked so far in one day! Only woman in elder group who never dropped out.

Each rest stop became torturous as leg muscles tightened. I retire fairly early for next morning's journey.

Saturday—July 15, 1978

The day has arrived! The day we descend upon Washington, D.C., believe it or not—my body is not as stiff or painful from yesterday's twenty-two miles. Once we begin the march, the muscles feel better. Still a good cloud cover today. March with the elders again. Great excitement and joy to see brothers and sisters for the historic event, and uniting in solidarity for Native issues and concerns.

Helicopters swooping low over the marchers—picture taking? The copters come again and again.

Malcolm X Park Rally
Phillip Deere offers prayer in Muscogee language.

General Assembly Monday—July 17, '78

About one-mile hike through beautiful woodland trail to primitive amphitheater. Headmen of 6 Nations all present at stage—wearing feathered headdresses—(reminds me of pics of Creek & Yuchi in early 1800s). Ribbon shirts abound—exquisite beadwork.

Chief Powless—6 Nations Oneida language and prayers. Audrey Shenandoah interpreter: 'We give greetings and thanksgiving.' Head Chief Oren Lyons.

Overview of Sunday'[s] discussion.

Elders' Council formation

Select Elder to represent group at Council

Social Dance tonight after

To gather support of non-Indian brothers—conduct ourselves in respectful way—do not order people—speak kindly to media & press. We are representing all people in camp. Conduct ourselves in a good way. Concern for elders must be transportation, food, water—humidity gets to elders.

Wed.—July 19

Philip Deere—Muscogee

Issues of N.A. Beginning of involvement outside of own community—met others who had similar problems.

Treatment, suffering same as others / mine. Police brutality same in our community.

Due to color / denied jobs.

Young Indian people fight for rights today.

Radicals—defending home, family.

Militant—is a wounded animal violent when cornered?

Divide & conquer system

Small jobs / funding—is there any future for our NA?

Other walks? We have walked long enough.

I don't want my children to come to this area.

Ashamed that NA must go to Geneva in behalf of Human Rights.

Perhaps we need to go to Germany.

Perhaps we need to remind Pres. Carter to look in his own backyard.

Just Leave It Till Morning

The following recollection illustrates how casually our older Euchee would move through, or interact with, a world of unseen Spirits, taking care not to "disturb things that should be left alone after dark." There was no fear or apprehension of this world, just acceptance, even humor. It's just the way things were. This was true whether we talk about our old ceremonial people or those who were members at our small Euchee churches. Sometimes fiction can create the feeling of how we go through this world. Other times, as with the story below, small everyday real occurrences between us and our elders best illustrate this world of ours.

One night my wife Dawn and I were sitting at home when "one of us" spilled something on the floor. It was just a small mess, not much really. She started to get the broom to sweep it up when she stopped and kind of laughed. She said "Umm!! Maggie and Josephine would be shaking their heads and telling me I shouldn't sweep after dark!"

I laughed and nodded, "Yes. Yes, they would."

Maggie and Josephine were my mother's relations, second cousins, I think. My mother's name was Josephine, too, but we called her Golaha (Grandmother), though most of her relations and the other Euchee her age tended to call her "Jo." All three of those old women spoke fluent

Euchee, and all are deceased. Maggie was a few years older than my mom, and Josephine was a few years younger than my mother. Maggie, Josephine, and my mom grew up together. When they were young, in their teens and early twenties, the three of them had played softball for Pickett Chapel, the small Euchee Methodist church, located five miles south of Sapulpa. They would sometimes talk about traveling to the other Indian churches to play their ball teams, remembering who played what positions. My mom had moved away when she got married, but Maggie and Josephine both lived their whole lives in and around Sapulpa and were lifelong members of Pickett Chapel.

My mother grew up speaking Euchee, not learning to speak English until she was five or six and started school. She continued speaking Euchee at home till she went off to college in 1940. After she married my dad in the 1950s, they moved away, and her fluency slowly dropped, but she could still speak Euchee well. However, by the time they moved back to Sapulpa in the late 1980s, she sometimes would pause for just a moment to think what to say next in Euchee. I grew up knowing some words and perhaps a few phrases. But Mom loved her language, so in 1990, my mother and I decided to start a Euchee-language class. I wanted to be serious about the language, I didn't want us to just learn how to count to ten, to teach the colors, or name the animals and birds. I wanted to learn how to speak, how to talk with each other. At that point, my mother didn't feel comfortable being the teacher for the Euchee class. Luckily, in the early 1990s, we still had a number of fluent speakers, probably several dozens. All the speakers were about my mother's age, in their seventies or older. My mom's cousin Josephine was one of the youngest fluent speakers.[1] My mom and I talked about who would be a good choice to teach our class. I also visited several of my mother's fluent relations about who they thought might be a good fit to teach our Euchee class.

At one time, the Euchee had three, maybe four, different communities spread over what are now Creek and Tulsa Counties, in the areas south and west of Tulsa, Oklahoma: Polecat, Duck Creek, Gypsy, and/or Big Pond. These are where the Euchee allotments had been loosely grouped in 1906, though most of those allotments are sold off now. Many Euchee still live around these areas, in the small towns like Bristow, Sapulpa, Kellyville, or Liberty Mounds. We are all related, have a common history and a common language, but settled in slightly different areas, the places we had settled in after we were removed here in the 1830s from the East.

Each community had, perhaps, a slightly different dialect or pattern when they spoke. It was minor; for instance, the Big Pond community might end a word with a long "e," whereas Polecat Euchee might end the word with a long "a." Sometimes, one community would use a slightly different word for something. When our class started, our elder speakers might, for instance, come up with different ways to translate "window." But there was nothing that would slow down speech or understanding among us, it was more of an accent than a dialect difference. And, of course, our language has different pronouns for women and men speakers, which could sometimes get mixed up for men or women if they were raised by the opposite gender.

As I asked around about finding a teacher during the early weeks of 1990, Maggie's name kept being mentioned as someone who spoke Euchee really well. Everyone agreed that if she said a word a certain way in Euchee, that was one right way to say it. There might be another way to pronounce or say the word, but Maggie's would be one correct way. So I asked Maggie if she would teach our class. She reluctantly agreed on the condition that I would lead the class and she would act as the "expert," as she would say with her self-deprecating laugh. With that, we were off and running with our Euchee-language classes. Josephine, along with some dozen other fluent speakers, regularly or semiregularly attended our classes. As our classes went along and I wanted to acquire more materials, I ended up visiting Josephine quite a bit to learn and fill in my knowledge.

Maggie had two sisters; everyone called them the Cumseh girls due to their maiden name, even when the three of them were in their seventies. They all encouraged me to learn, always speaking to me in Euchee, teasing me about words I would forget, like "gravy," *dzoka-dzosha*. They would greet me in Euchee, then say *dzoka-dzosha* with a slight smile. It made them happy to see young people interested in our language. They loved hearing and speaking Euchee and wanted to see it continue.

Josephine's Uncle Max lived with her, with them speaking Euchee together every day. I'm not sure how old Max was, but he was old, probably in his late eighties or early nineties when I got to know him. Josephine said after Max had retired, when he was in his seventies and was living with Josephine, Max decided he was done speaking English, he had spoken it long enough. It was just Euchee for him after that. Over the few years I knew Max, I never heard him speak English. Maybe that's why Josephine spoke Euchee so well, really well, and fast. Or so it seemed to me. I loved listening to those elders speaking Euchee. They had a natural cadence, a rhythm to their speech we English speakers learning Euchee have trouble duplicating. Their speech was like someone speaking prose, like water going down a stream, flowing into the listener.

I would visit Josephine at her house, just a few miles south of Sapulpa, the area we call Pickett Prairie. Sometimes my mother would come along, and they would visit together in Euchee while I listened and tried to participate as best I could. The area Josephine lived in was still rural, part of her father's or grandfather's original allotment. Her uncle had been an Indian doctor, and a small old wooden shed was still standing in the back where he fixed medicines for people. A few years before I started visiting them at their old place, the Creek Nation had built Josephine a new house next to the one her grandfather built. The new house was a typical one-story brick Indian housing unit you see all across Oklahoma. The old wooden house was still there, though it was in rough shape. The old home had broken windows; faded, chipped paint; and a leaking roof. It did not look, and was not, livable.

In the mornings, Max would wake up in the new house, get his coffee, and then he would go next door to the old place and sit on the front steps of the old porch. When I would drive up to her house, there would be Max sitting at the old home with his coffee, his ball cap slightly skewed on his head. He would smile and wave, and then I would go in the new house to visit with Josephine. He would sit there most of the day, at that home, where he had lived all those years, next to the nice new house the Creek Nation built. That's how I always think of Max, sitting at that old home. Occasionally, when visiting Josephine, I would ask her about a Euchee word or phrase that she was not sure about. She would say, "Umm, I don't know about that. Let me ask Max," then get up and head out the door to find her uncle.

I can still hear his old-style Euchee speech, no abbreviations, no choppiness to his speech. The younger generation sometimes abbreviated those Euchee words. Particles would get dropped off of words, pieces that aren't really needed but give nuance and flavor to the words, slipping away from the old way of speaking. Another one of my mother's elder cousins, who grew up with his very old father, always first taught the full, old word, explaining that once you know the whole word, then you know what is missing, what is meant. His dad, born in the 1860s, had said the younger generation talked a funny Euchee because of that, the dropping of particles—abbreviations. His dad was referring to those Euchee who were born in or around the 1920s, who were all very fluent speakers.

Sometime around the year 2000, Pickett Chapel received a grant to hold sewing classes, to buy a few sewing machines and pay someone as an instructor for the class. Rev. Foot asked my wife if she could teach the class, as at the time Dawn was doing a lot of quilting and sewing. She was a bit nervous but was happy to help out. They held the sewing classes in the afternoon at Pickett Chapel, there south of Sapulpa. The classes started out with a handful of women attending. After a while, though, it was usually just Maggie and Josephine who came, with my mother or someone else occasionally attending the sewing class. Dawn would show them how to do stitches or help with a new pattern. Maggie and Josephine spoke with each other in Euchee while they sewed, visiting and laughing.

They'd pause occasionally, dropping into English, to tell my wife, "Don't worry, we're not talking about you!"

Dawn would laugh and respond, "I'm not worried, I can't understand anyway."

At one of the sewing classes that my mother came to, she was telling Maggie and Josephine how the night before my dad made a mess by spilling something on the floor. Mom went on as to how she had to look for the broom and dustpan to sweep it up.

Maggie and Josephine looked at my mom and in unison said, "Oh . . ." They made those little *tsk-tsk* noises with their slight smiles and shook their heads.

"Oh, I never sweep up at night. It can just wait till morning," Maggie said.

"I know, but sometimes I just go ahead and sweep it up," my mom answered.

Josephine said, "Well, I just leave it till morning. If it's a mess, sometimes I put a rag or a tea towel over it." Laughing, she added, "Then I take care of it in the morning."

All three of those Euchee women laughed about that. Maggie turned to Dawn and explained, "We never used to sweep or rake up anything at night. You don't want to disturb things that should be left alone after dark. You just don't do it." For them, it wasn't the mess that would be disturbed, but the things, the Spirits, one didn't see that one would chase around with the broom or the rake after dusk. I am sure they didn't even think about it, but if asked, perhaps they would talk about

how there are always Spirits around, even when you don't know it. That
is just the way things were in their world.

We Euchee still have big things like our Green Corn ceremonies,
funerals, and so forth that have been handed to us from long ago. However, it's these little things that one simply does without thinking that
make our life unique and full. Those elderly women, those church
women, believed in their Euchee language and their Euchee ways. It's
little things like a mess on the floor at night "that can just wait till morning" that will suddenly remind us of those old Euchee women and what
they brought to this world.

Wild Onion Dinners

In Creek and Euchee Country, starting in late February and early
March, we start thinking about the wild onions growing throughout eastern Oklahoma. I'm not sure other tribes have them as
ingrained in their rites of spring as we do. I hear of some onion dinners
in Cherokee or Choctaw country, sometimes even toward Oklahoma
City. But for Euchee and Creeks, we plan our Saturdays around wild
onion dinners for the six to eight weeks they are in season—a small but
significant way of life for Euchee and Creeks, no less than attending
ball tournaments or pow-wows for other Indians. Every weekend come
March and most of April, some Creek or Euchee Indian church, or
maybe Indian community, hosts a fund-raiser wild onion dinner. Often
several dinners occur at the same time, and then we have to decide
which one we'll go to, as in, "Salt Creek's is so good, but we don't feel
like driving all the way down there, so we'll probably just go over toward
Broken Arrow." Or, "They're having one over there, but last year they
ran out of onions early, so we don't know where we'll go." Wild onion
dinners often form one of the year's major fund-raisers for some Indian
churches, and they go all out for them. It takes a lot of work, as just
getting the gallons and gallons of wild onions takes coordinating.

Wild onions start sprouting down south, that is, in the southern part
of the Creek Nation, as early as late January if there has been some rain
and warm weather. Usually, though, it is more like mid or late February. The tender little green shoots start appearing in clearings, often
along or close to streams. Some of our relations and friends depend on

Wild onion dinner: corn, pinto beans, fry bread,
salt meat, wild onions in egg.

picking and selling the onions they gather to supplement their income. During early spring, you'll hear a knock on the door, and someone will be there saying, "Momma said you might want some onions." They usually sell a quart for $10, or maybe $25 for a gallon, already cleaned and cut, packed in clear plastic food bags. If it's one of your relations that's been drinking a bunch, the onions might not be cleaned so well, the onions may still have some of the dirt from the earth where they were dug up, but they're probably cheap. You can tell good onions from the next room, even through the baggies they smell strong. When someone finds a good spot where the onions really grow, they tend to visit it year after year, careful not to pick it clean so the onions will return. Most of us know better than to even ask where they picked their onions; at best you will get a nondescript "Oh, over toward Bristow." Or maybe a "by Kellyville" or "down south." More likely, you will get no response, maybe a laugh or just a look. One doesn't give up information on how to find one's wild onion patch.

Most of us have our favorite wild onion dinners we try to go to every year. Maybe because of the food, or because they serve all you can eat, or we want to support their fund-raising efforts. Or maybe because we will see our friends and relations there. Probably a combination of the above. The food for the dinners centers on the wild onions cooked with eggs, at least within our territory. I've heard that some other places cook them in gravy, which I cannot imagine. I guess to each their own, but one would get a strange, distant look if that was tried at one of the Creek or Euchee dinners. Depending on where you go, the other staples include ham, salt meat, sometimes fried chicken, pinto beans, corn or green beans, fry bread, and sometimes cornbread, almost always *sofki*, a traditional kind of drink made with *sofki* corn cooked with lye (made by pouring water through hickory ashes). Some of the full-blood old timers liked their *sofki* sour, a trait I never ever acquired. My aunt Maxine used to always have a small mason jar with lye in her cupboard, and if she ran out, she would ask us if we knew someone that made or had extra lye. The onion dinners also usually have a simple salad, and for desserts: sheet cakes, pies, and probably cobblers, grape dumplings (a traditional Creek and Euchee dessert made with grape juice and dumplings, which used to be made with wild grapes). Sometimes they have blue dumplings (another traditional Creek and Euchee dessert) if they have old women cooks. For drinks, it's iced tea and coffee. Always coffee. Then, depending on where you are, you may get extra choices like chicken and dumplings, vegetable beef soup, spaghetti or goulash, baked beans, and if I am lucky and they have some old women cooking— sour cornbread.

If you go to the Indian churches whose membership still includes old Creeks or Euchee, you count on those traditional extra dishes, *sofki*, grape dumplings, sour cornbread. With so much intermarriage with non-Indians, not all those old foods get passed along to the younger generation. I have occasionally seen *obvske* at a dinner, a drink made with parched, finely ground cornmeal. Few people make that, and fewer share it. In Euchee, we call it *chi῀ch'a*, and we would add a teaspoon of sugar to it. Except during our Green Corn, or when we visit our friends' ceremonies or funerals, onion dinners are about the only time I eat salt meat. I can always tell it is that time of year because come Monday morning, my fingers will be swollen and puffy from eating all that salt meat. It is not the time to get your regular medical checkup, because all the health numbers will be in the red. But some traditions have to be carried on regardless of the cost.

Salt Creek Indian Methodist Church, by Holdenville, always has one of the biggest and best onion dinners. We went there a few times, but it has been some years since we last went. It is probably a seventy-five-minute drive from Sapulpa, and the lines are usually long. But it is worth the drive, and the lines move quickly. And the food was always so good, those Creek women down there can really cook. However, nowadays we stay closer to home. We usually end up going to Concharty's or Haikey Chapel's dinners, both also Indian Methodist churches.

Concharty is just a few miles east and south of Duck Creek stomp grounds, just three or four miles north of Highway 16. Concharty is a mile down a gated gravel, or poorly maintained paved, road. There is not much else out there. Like so many Indian places, one does not find it by accident. They always have a huge choice and all you can eat. One needs to get there early, or you end up parking on the road, even with as much space as they have. We, of course, know members there and love supporting them and visiting. Concharty is located on a few acres of land and still has several family camp houses located around the church. Some of the members do their cooking for the dinner at these camp houses, bringing the food up to the fellowship hall for the visitors. The line for food winds out the door, down the side of the fellowship hall. But, again, it moves quickly, and one passes the time visiting the others standing there with you. The fellowship hall has maybe four rows of three folding tables each eight feet long. You load up your Styrofoam plate with onions, salt meat, and whatever you can fit on the plate and then try to find a spot to sit together. But they can seat a lot of people. It is always noisy and busy, visiting with friends one has not seen in a while, and planning things with those relations one sees every few weeks. And of course kids are running back and forth. Sometimes after they quickly eat, you don't see your little ones till you hunt them down to leave, finding them running with the other kids, their cousins or "new friends."

Haikey Chapel is the other onion dinner we always try to make. Haikey is now in what has become South Tulsa, just off of Memorial on 101st Street. Only twenty or thirty years ago it was still a mostly rural area. My friend whose family has been members there since its founding in the late 1800s talks about how she remembers that they used to haul spring water from a well by the chapel for cooking and drinking. Now Haikey has housing additions, movie theaters, and car dealerships next door, even a Super Target just a quarter mile away. I'm not sure you could find the old spring, let alone that it would be safe to drink from it. The well, much like many of our ways, has been paved over, not seen, forgotten about. The chapel sits back from the road a bit and still has a little space left with plenty of parking. A spot of old rural Indian Country in the midst of South Tulsa. Probably most of the white people zipping by on the road never even notice the small Indian church that still holds on.

My dad, who passed away around 2008, used to preach at Haikey for a few years and fill in at other times. The Oklahoma Indian Missionary Conference of the Methodist Church was always short of ministers, depending on lay preachers for regular services, so when they needed an ordained minister who could serve communion, my dad was often called upon to serve. We would take my mom, who passed away in 2016, whenever we went to their onion dinner. She enjoyed visiting because of my dad's tie to the church, but also because she grew up in these little Indian churches, including Haikey. She knew all the older members, or the members' parents, grandparents, or uncles and aunts. She would talk about attending church there or playing ball against the other church girls back in the 1930s. Those last few years it seemed like we always ran into Aunt Martha at Haikey. She was actually mom's cousin who was taken in by my mom's grandmother when Martha's dad passed away and Martha's mom left. My mother's grandmother raised a bunch of her grandkids in the 1920s and '30s, and they were more like siblings than cousins. Martha's granddaughter was always taking Aunt Martha around to places, just like we did with my mom. Martha was maybe a few years younger than my mom, and both were full-blood Euchee and fluent speakers, some of our last native fluent Euchee speakers. I always tried to pay for their dinners, it wasn't much, maybe eight or ten dollars, but it made me happy to do something for Aunt Martha and my cousin, as they always came to check on and visit my mother. Martha and my mom would sit there in Haikey's fellowship hall on those hard steel folding chairs and visit, slowly eating their food. They'd greet and visit people they knew, and they both knew so many people over their ninety-plus years of living in the Creek and Euchee communities. They would talk in Euchee to each other, in that rising and falling cadence that only those old ones had to their language, like a breeze rippling through the trees, while eating their wild onions and chewing on salt meat. I could sometimes follow what they said, sometimes pretty well, talking about places and people. Aunt Martha, though, talked fast, and when the words poured out, I could get lost translating in my mind the sentences she had said, quickly falling behind what they were talking about.

Years before at an onion dinner at Duck Creek Community (which is mostly Euchee) when our youngest daughter, who is now in her thirties, was only five or six months old, Aunt Martha was there, and we sat together. Dawn had told Martha that the "baby was sobby" because she was teething. Aunt Martha gave our daughter some salt meat, saying the salt meat would be good for that, it would give her something to chew on and soothe her gums. Dawn was holding her breath thinking our baby was going to choke or all the salt would be bad for her, but afraid to say anything to the little full-blood Euchee great auntie. Aunt Martha just gave that quiet almost laugh all those old Euchee women seemed to have, saying, "Babies like to suck on the rind, it makes their gums feel better." And our daughter did, she gnawed on that piece till it was soft and mushy and fell apart. When we tried to take what was left from her, she got mad, and we had to get her another piece.

The last onion dinner we took my mom to was at Haikey. We went a little later than usual because the older mom got, the longer it took to get her ready and out the door. At ninety-plus years old, one does not get hurried along. She always spent time on her hair. We knew that was one thing she didn't like about aging; she always had such full, thick black hair, and in the last few years it was thinning and more brittle. Still full, but one pays a price for living so long. So, we gave her time. But she always looked forward to going to those dinners, so we made an effort to take her, even if it took twice as long for us to get ready. When we got to Haikey, there was still something of a line out the door of the fellowship hall. They had put up a large ten-by-twenty-foot pop-up arbor or tent next to the hall to cook in, as the hall did not have enough space to do all the food preparation. Plus, the hall would overheat, even in the occasionally cold weather of March. Our friend was in there cooking, maybe frying bread or fixing the onions. As soon as she saw us standing there, she came out and greeted my mom, "How are you, Miss Josephine?" and then moved us to the front of the line— one of the perks of being with the oldest woman by a decade at the dinner. We visited with our friend for a moment as I paid the preacher for our meals and then told my mom to go sit down while we got her food. The wild onions, as always, looked perfectly cooked, not too much egg, not overcooked. My mom, of course, was visiting people as our friend helped mom find three seats together for us. I'm not sure now, but I suspect someone probably got up and offered her their seat as they "were finished anyway." Everyone fully respected age within our communities and were always proud to see our elders out and about. And my mother enjoyed being there. She got sad sometimes about having out-lived all the people that she had grown up with, but being in a place she remembered from her youth, inside that hall, brought back fond memories and comfort. It might be surrounded by white peoples' development, but inside that hall with pictures of all the Old People on the walls it was still Indian Country, filled with our history.

As my mother slowly finished her meal, visiting with us and others, one of the church members came up and asked her what she wanted for dessert. Pie? Cobbler? Cake? Grape dumplings? She wanted pecan pie. The church member said she would get the dessert for Mom. She went up to the dessert table and got her a piece of pie, came back, and set it in front of Mom.

My mom said, "Thank you" and looked at it for a moment and then said, "Where's the ice cream?"

My wife told her, "They don't have ice cream, Golaha."

Mom looked at the pie and at us and said, "You always have ice cream with pie."

Our granddaughter, who was about ten at the time, was getting embarrassed. Since my mom couldn't hear that well, she tended to speak louder than others, and everyone around us could hear her. Our friend was still standing there, and looking bemused by the whole thing, having known my mom since before she could remember.

My mom said, again, "I thought there would be ice cream with the pie."

Our friend laughed and said, "Let me go see, Miss Josephine," and went to the refrigerator-freezer at the front of the fellowship hall. As it turned out, there was some vanilla ice cream left over from a social the church had held a couple of months earlier. She grabbed a scoop, got a little bowl and brought my mom some ice cream for her pie and told her, "There you go, Josephine."

My mom smiled and told her, "Thank you," and happily ate her dessert.

Our friend laughed and told us, "We're happy to do anything we can do to keep our elders happy!"

That was the last time my mom went to a wild onion dinner. So many little things like those fund-raisers that one doesn't think about at the time as being much of anything, which over time, make up what we miss most. Those months before Mom passed away, she got tired so easily that it was hard to take her to visit. But we were lucky to go to all those Indian churches and places with Mom, Aunt Martha, and other friends and relations. Now, because of Covid over the last few years, so many onion dinners have been cancelled or are just "take out" or "to go" that we've missed visiting people. We look forward to again having puffy fingers on Mondays from too much salt meat, catching up with those we have not seen during the winter months, and remembering those who have gone on.

Bill and I Go to the
Supreme Court

I practiced law with my friend G. William Rice for many years, working together on projects even after he transitioned to full-time law professor in the mid- to late 1990s. I graduated from law school in 1985, and then had a fellowship for a year at the University of Wisconsin, getting my LL.M. in 1987. By then, Bill had been practicing for seven or eight years. He had been in partnership with Browning Pipestem, who graduated from law school in 1968. Browning spent time in the early 1970s as an attorney with the Department of the Interior and Native American Rights Fund before returning to practice in Oklahoma. Together and individually, Browning and Bill were two giants of Indian law. They were instrumental in getting tribal courts up and running in Oklahoma in the late 1970s and early 1980s. When I started lawyering in the mid-1980s, they had gone their separate ways, Browning staying in Norman, Oklahoma, and Bill, who was enrolled with the United Keetowah Band of Cherokees, living with his Sauk wife and children in Cushing, Oklahoma, working for the Sac and Fox Nation.

Cushing, with a population of about eight thousand, was on the northern edge of Sac and Fox territory and still had numerous Sauk allotments. It was a small town that used to have a thriving oil business. Cushing still has one of the United States' largest oil storage capacities, with huge oil tanks surrounding the town capable of holding somewhere between 75 and 90 million barrels of oil. After working several places the first few years after I graduated, I ended up with Bill, working out of his small downtown Cushing office. Though, at that

Poster for Sac and Fox Nation Victory Day, annual celebration
of their Supreme Court case.

time, there was not much of a downtown to Cushing, probably more
empty storefronts and office windows than occupied spaces.

In Oklahoma, the CFR courts and tribal courts were resurrected in
1978, some forty-five years ago. More precisely, Courts of Indian
Offences, operated by the Bureau of Indian Affairs (BIA) on behalf of
tribes who lack a tribal court. Like everything in Indian Country, even
the acronyms do not have a straightforward story. The source of authority for the BIA courts is found in the Code of Federal Regulations, and
thus these are referred to as CFR courts. The CFRs commenced
because *State v. Littlechief* (1978) held that Kiowa allotments were Indian
Country, and therefore the state of Oklahoma was without criminal
jurisdiction. Browning Pipestem filed the amicus briefs in the state and
federal *Littlechief* cases, which the courts acknowledged as "the excellent briefs filed by Mr. F. Browning Pipestem and Mr. William Doug-
las Giessmann on behalf of United Indian Tribes of Western Oklahoma
and Kansas." G. William Rice was a law clerk at the Oklahoma Court

of Criminal Appeals, which adopted the federal court ruling. Sonny Chibitty was another Native attorney who, along with Browning, Bill, and Phil Lujan, helped get the first CFR courts up and running. I don't know what became of Mr. Giessmann, though another attorney friend vaguely remembers him.

I didn't know Sonny, though I got to know Sonny's father, Charles Chibitty, when Charles would bring a granddaughter he was raising to the same Tulsa gymnastics gym that my daughter attended. Sonny's dad and I would visit, he sharing stories about his time as a Comanche Code Talker in World War II. Charles's daughter was also an attorney but passed away sometime in the early 1990s. I later learned that in the 1980s, Pam was chief of the Loyal Shawnee Tribe, now known as the Shawnee Tribe, for which I have worked. Like so much of Indian Country, personal connections make for a small, interconnected community. All those great lawyers, except Phil, are gone. Phil Lujan, the first CFR prosecutor for the resurrected Oklahoma tribal jurisdiction, still works as a tribal judge in Oklahoma, bringing his own particular Kiowa personality to the matters before him. I have spent years appearing in various tribal courts with, or as a judge alongside, Judge Lujan, including Seminole Nation CFR, Citizen Potawatomi, Kickapoo Tribe of Oklahoma, Sac and Fox, and Kansas Kickapoo. Now, most tribes have transitioned from CFR to tribal courts. However, it's important to remember that when *Littlechief* was argued in the 1970s, tribal sovereignty and jurisdiction in Oklahoma was not a sure thing. Sovereignty is not given. It does not happen without work and planning. And it does not live without vision. It is also a story often driven by dedicated individual Natives purposefully working within Indian Country. Without *Littlechief*, the recent *McGirt* Supreme Court decision finding that the Muscogee Nation reservation continued to exist would not have happened, with its exponential increase in tribal court caseload.

Probably Bill's biggest career moment, with me alongside even if only to carry the briefcase, was to litigate, appeal, argue, and ultimately win by unanimous decision the U.S. Supreme Court case *Oklahoma Tax Commission v. Sac and Fox Nation*, 508 U.S. 114 (1993). The case concerned the Sac and Fox assertion that tribes were exempt from state taxation on their automobiles garaged on tribal lands. Auto license plates are the proof that a vehicle is properly tagged and taxed within a jurisdiction. On May 17, 1993, G. William and I heard we won in the Supreme Court, and that day is now memorialized by the Sac and Fox as Victory Day, an official Sauk holiday. The case is in every Indian law casebook, and it is why you see tribal license plates throughout Oklahoma. G. William Rice argued the case, with me sitting in the second chair. Second chair is like the backup quarterback, ready to act if the big name can't appear. Luckily, I never had to step in for Bill. Truman Carter, the elected treasurer on the Sac and Fox's Business Committee, sat in the third chair at the Supreme Court. We believed that was the first time, and perhaps the only time, the three counsel chairs at a Supreme Court argument were filled by enrolled tribal members.

Nowadays, most Indian lawyers know Professor Rice from his teaching at the Pre-Law Summer Institute (PLSI), which prepares Native college graduates for law school, or from being Professor Rice at Tulsa Law School. I knew him as an extraordinary lawyer and friend. We litigated and briefed, and Bill argued the tag case, through the federal courts to the Supreme Court, with the ultimate unanimous nine-to-zero win. The SFN is not a large tribe, maybe some three thousand members during the time of the litigation, but its leadership understood that the cost of sovereignty is support, belief, and determination. The months leading to the oral argument were intense, challenging, obsessed. Bill was at his brilliant best thinking and writing after midnight. Many nights I would leave the Cushing office at 4:00 A.M. for the drive home to Sapulpa while Bill worked away, often till daylight. Then back to the office around noon to start all over.

I would drive State Highway 48 from small-city Sapulpa to small-town Cushing through rural countryside, seeing the fields filled with wildflowers, rivers, and woods. There was always wildlife, too, deer, sometimes wild turkeys, even once or twice a bobcat. Along the way, I would think how this forty-minute drive was so different from that of most of my classmates who worked at the mega firms, with their forty-five or sixty-minute, maybe even longer, commute on the subways or overbuilt highways of New York City, Washington, D.C., Chicago, and other big cities. Every day I traveled from Euchee Country to Sac and Fox territory, past the Walmart, past my mom's old cousins' houses, the dirt road turnoff going to Polecat stomp grounds and old Euchee allotments. I passed through the dried-up oil boomtown of Drumright, whose population exploded in the mid-1910s to around fifteen thousand, with supposedly more millionaires per capita than anywhere in the United States. Most of Drumright was in Creek County and thus within the Creek Nation, though the reservation status was still decades from reaffirmation. The western edge of Drumright was in Sac and Fox country, including the golf course, which was on a Sac and Fox allotment. While researching a lawsuit we filed in Sac and Fox tribal court to impose taxes on oil operators on Sac and Fox allotments, I found one Creek allotment in the Drumright area that around 1917 had some five thousand barrels of oil pumped per day from it. I always thought those Creek Indians with all that oil pumped probably had no money left by the time of the Depression, having either lost, stolen, or misspent it. Back in those days, the only ones profiting off Creek and Euchee oil wells were usually the oil companies and the lawyers who represented the Indians in court to sign oil deals and leases.

Our office in Cushing was small, just Bill, me, and Bill's cousin Brent. Brent, who was also an attorney, helped and managed to keep alive our regular law practice, which was strictly tribal. Not a fancy, big, high-rolling law firm, just the three of us. Bill often in overalls and beat-up boots, with his rural Oklahoma drawl. I saw many very good elite firms make the mistake of assuming Bill was just a small-time hometown attorney. Those attorneys only got to make that mistake once. His sister Laurie helped as secretary/receptionist, and occasionally his wife Annette helped between watching their kids and going off to pow-wows on the weekends. Bill's kids spent hours playing at the office, a family affair. We would have various Sauk citizens stop by, including Bill's father-in-law and Annette's grandma Oma. They were both Sauk speakers and traditional Sauk practitioners. Those elements flowed through our office and our work. We also had a Creek woman who had worked with Bill as his secretary, receptionist, and office manager. I think she was a few years older than Bill and was very sweet. Sometimes, though, Brent and I would laugh because she seemed to forget Brent and I were also attorneys in the office, as we watched her bring Bill a coffee and then hurry past us standing there with empty cups. Regardless, we all put in the hours to get things done.

I hope that new Indian lawyers are blessed to have weeks like ours leading up to the Supreme Court oral argument on March 23, 1993. It was as good as law practice gets. Thinking, analyzing, working through possibilities, consumed with winning for the tribe. The week our final brief was due at the Supreme Court meant long hours. This was before emails and the internet were really a thing, and to the extent they existed, they were so very slow. Dial tones and a dedicated phone line for the internet was a luxury. We had to get our briefs drafted, faxed off to the specialized court printers in D.C., then wait for them to fax their draft print back to us for our review and edits, and then we had to fax it back to them. Once we had what was our best final draft faxed to the printer, we had to anxiously wait for word that the printer had filed the brief and all copies with the Supreme Court before the Court closed for the day. Then we just had to wait and prepare for the big day.

Bill and I drove out to Washington, D.C., from Oklahoma for the arguments. We left sometime late afternoon, with him picking me up in Sapulpa on his way from Cushing. We probably were supposed to leave earlier in the day, but as usual I didn't really expect Bill till evening. I don't even remember where we stayed on the drive, or if we even drove straight through. I mostly remember drinking coffee along the way. At one stop to get coffee somewhere on I-40 in Arkansas, we laughed about kicking the empty coffee cups and Barbie dolls from underfoot as we got out of the car. Remarking how when we were younger, it would have been empty beer cans we stepped on. Driving that night, we went over what might be asked and how he should respond. Bill had the best grasp and understanding of Indian case law of anyone I have ever known. He could remember case names, holdings, and even the citations from the dozens, maybe hundreds of cases we'd read. However, Bill was also wanting to build a log home in Cushing on his wife's family Sauk allotment, so on the way to D.C. we made a few detours to check out log-home building suppliers. So, here we were, a couple of long-haired Indian lawyers on their way to argue in the U.S. Supreme Court, making repeated stops to wander around Tennessee log yards and antique tool stores. It was always an adventure with Bill.

Once in D.C., we were fortunate to have the Sonosky, Chambers, and Sachse law firm lend us their offices to prepare for our argument. That firm represented tribal clients, and we were friends with several of their attorneys, all experienced, excellent lawyers. They also helped by running through moot arguments with Bill, peppering him with questions they thought the Court might ask, and Bill having an answer for everything they threw at him. As we left nothing to chance, on the Monday before our argument we toured the Supreme Court building so we would be familiar with the physical layout of the courtroom. Unsurprisingly, Bill knew one of the court clerks, not one of the justices' clerks, but the ones who handle the filings and administrative work, who was kind enough to give us a behind-the-scenes look. One does not realize how very small, so tiny, the actual courtroom is till seen. The heavy, deep red drapes hanging from the ceiling, the dark wooden justices' bench, counsel tables and chairs, white marble pillars. It left a clear impression of seriousness and power contained within the courtroom. It is the judicial throne room of an empire not always friendly to tribes.

We stayed at a hotel just south of where the National Museum of the American Indian now stands, nice but not fancy, within walking distance of the Capitol. I don't remember, but I imagine we took a cab to the Court the morning of the arguments. The day went well, very well. We were ushered into the courtroom, seated in chairs just behind the counsel table, as there was a case being argued just before us. We were seated there like an on-deck batter at a ballgame. When our case came up, we were directed to move up to the counsel table, with the quill feather pen laid there for each of us, a traditional memento of our appearing before the Court. Bill made as fine an oral presentation as I have ever heard. Bill argued at the podium, maybe six or eight feet from the Justices, with me in the second chair, Truman next to me in the third chair. Truman was the one who actually got ticketed and his car impounded by Lincoln County for having those red-and-white SFN license plates on his vehicle, "illegal tribal tags." Truman got the entire case started, which led us to be sitting that March day in front of the United States Supreme Court. Bill's oral presentation was intense and effective.

After everyone—the Oklahoma Tax Commission, Bill, and the Solicitor General on the side of the tribe—made their presentations, we exited the court. We visited in front of the Court with the Sauk officials, some of the other Indian lawyers, and others who had attended the oral arguments. When that was over with, just Bill and I went to get a cup of coffee, I think at one of the coffeeshops in the Congressional buildings, as this was before all the security was in place after 9/11. I had a picture of that moment post-argument, Bill looking absolutely, totally drained, nothing left, having poured his all into preparations and argument.

Over the years, we talked about those times. The long nights researching, writing, discussing, how we would be happy to just do Supreme Court advocacy for the remainder of our careers, like oral advocacy monks, cloistered in a world of Indian law arguments. Our win and the time spent with Bill at the Federal Tenth Circuit Court of Appeals and Supreme Court was one of the most rewarding, amazing, fun periods in my legal career. Bill and I both looked forward to going back to the Supreme Court to argue for tribes, but that unfortunately never happened. I never understood why no tribe ever again used Bill to argue their cases, as he was one of the very brightest minds and oral advocates in Indian Country. He was disappointed about it, especially after he claimed that Supreme Court advocates were allowed to wear formal morning day dress to argue. I never verified the morning wear fact, but Bill was seldom wrong. He was dying to wear that formal tux. I am sure if we had, we would have ended up with the top hats, too. It was the tribes' loss not to utilize Bill's extraordinary intellect and advocacy skills, too often relying on non-Indian hired guns. For at least an eighteen-year period, 2004 to 2022, no Indian law case was argued on behalf of the tribes by a Native American attorney. Sometimes in law, just as in fiction, who tells the story matters.

Tribes still need that intensity from their advocates. Bill had a vision of where Indians could and should go. Tribes not utilizing him in the Supreme Court was a loss for Indian Country, not only in terms of lost decisions but in lost examples of what Indians could do. Storytelling has many uses for Native Americans. Brother Bill was so very good at telling his stories in a judicial world, showing what we could be and how to get there. Big wins for Native Americans in the Supreme Court have been few since then. I hope Indian Country keeps arguing for their rights, and I hope that when the cases matter most, they use some of the brilliant talent they produce.

That period leaves me fond memories and missing my friend. I thought about those moments a year or two ago while eating lunch with friends at the Chicken Shack on Route 66 near Luther, Oklahoma, talking about tribal affairs and listening to them talk in Kickapoo. Spending time with those tribal officials, hearing a Native language still being used, and seeing their tribally tagged vehicles in the parking lot is why Bill and I got into the Indian law business. Small blessings remind me it is good to live and work in Indian Country.

Seven Thousand Dzogala

*The Native American Graves Protection and Repatriation Act
(NAGPRA) became law on November 16, 1990.[2] NAGPRA
seeks to protect Native American human remains, requiring federal
agencies and institutions that receive federal funding to return
Native American cultural items to lineal descendants and culturally affiliated American Indian tribes, Alaska Native villages, and
Native Hawaiians. This specifically includes human remains
and other cultural items such as funerary objects, sacred objects,
and objects of cultural patrimony. Those regulations are currently
under review, but the law remains.*

*I graduated from Harvard Law School in 1985. Since then, I
have almost exclusively practiced in the field of federal Indian law
or in tribal law. In my personal life, participation in my Euchee
traditional ceremonies shades everything I do. Our ceremonies
teach us that the spiritual and physical world merge, they are not
separated. Part of this is an awareness of those who have gone on,
our Ancestors. In one unique instance, traditional directives and
federal law merge.*

*Thus, it is a sad, bitter fact that my law school's parent institu-
tion, Harvard University, acquired thousands of Native American
human remains and many other Indigenous remains and cultural
items. Yet thirty years after NAGPRA, Harvard remained in possession of most of those thousands of tribal human remains. One of
the world's greatest academic institutions somehow did not have*

sufficient expertise or resources to interact with Indian tribes and return their stolen Ancestors, even when the site from which most of those remains were stolen was known down to the county from where they were taken. Throughout the 1990s, Harvard University Native American Program students raised concerns to the university about holding our Ancestors in the Peabody Museum.[3] So, Native Harvard University alumni once again put forward our concerns by letter to Harvard regarding this spectacular, ongoing failure to repatriate. It may be that the Peabody is now trying to make amends, albeit belatedly. Harvard released in September 2022 a report on slave and Native remains in the university's possession, which tried—but for many Native alumni failed—to make amends. Within weeks of the report's release, the Peabody had to admit to yet another transgression against our people, that it had hair samples taken in the 1930s from some six hundred children who were at Indian boarding schools. One of those children, I found out, was my aunt, married to my mother's younger brother. My aunt's three living children are now in their sixties and seventies. My cousins ultimately decided to simply have the Peabody respectfully dispose of her hair because they did not know how one deals with such items—what are the protocols for such transgressions? I had, and still have, a visceral, emotional, cultural reaction that needs expressing, one that fundamentally explains how Harvard and other institutions so morally failed in their obligations. Harvard, and too many other institutions, still fail to comprehend the depth of these wrongs. The obligations and duties cannot simply be passed down to one of their departments. NAGPRA indeed vests repatriation processes in tribes. However, the harm and trauma of stolen Ancestors housed in boxes deeply impacts Native students and alumni. Institutions seem unable, or unwilling, to acknowledge such personal wrongs beyond issuing a formulaic "land acknowledgment" before an institution's presentations. I pray this has changed since the first report, but my reaction to the news remains the same. This essay is my attempt to tell this in my own way, and perhaps to give some context to the stories that follow.

On behalf of the University, we apologize to those parties who will be negatively impacted by the draft [report's] premature release by the *Harvard Crimson* . . .[4]

That response, in regard to the *Harvard Crimson*'s release of a draft report by Harvard University on the human remains it holds of at least nineteen individuals who were likely enslaved and almost seven thousand Native American human remains that represent "the University's engagement and complicity" with slavery and colonialism.

"*Dzogala! Dzogala! Wafuhnji-jehn?*" *Sage wegwa-jehn.*

("My relations! My relations! Where did you go?" Bear asked.)

Sage (Bear) is the great lumbering friend of Shajwane (Rabbit). In our traditional Euchee stories, Bear and Rabbit are relations, *Dzogala,* cousins—relations. They call each other *digadi,* friends. These words have power; they have meaning. Sometimes Rabbit uses these words too casually, letting the listener know his character and that one should pay attention to what happens next. Sometimes these are just stories, sometimes they say things we cannot say for ourselves. In my recent story *The Last Old Woman,* I write about how Shajwane and his friends, representing our past, fade away when we fail to continue telling their stories, fail to continue our ways.[5] Now I realize they may also fade away when those Ancestors are not there to hear the stories, unable to hear because they are locked away in boxes, dug up and taken from the things that they carry to the other side; no longer tied to us spiritually, removed from place and people.

Harvard University, in its Peabody Museum of Archaeology and Ethnology, has *almost seven thousand* Native American remains—from the United States. It may have another sixteen thousand Indigenous people from around the world and perhaps nineteen slaves' remains. Still has them, thirty years after the passage of the federal Native American Graves Repatriation Act, which mandates the return of Native American remains from institutions that receive federal money: a sickening, disgusting fact about my law school's university. Perhaps it is because I write this having gotten home at 6:30 A.M. from our dance at Polecat, our main Euchee stomp grounds. I got to bed around 7:00 A.M., managing to sleep for some three hours before I got up again. Maybe I am tired. Worn out. But . . .

Seven thousand Ancestors.

This fact will not go away. I tried. I heard and read of those who may be working on the committee at Harvard to address this "issue." I started law school at Harvard forty years ago. I became a lawyer to help protect tribes and tribal people from abuse, from destruction of their lands; to protect their tribal ways. The federal law directing the return of our Ancestors has been around almost as long as I have been a lawyer. So I cannot accept the request for patience from those involved.

Paige, my chief at our ceremonial grounds and of our religion, stopped over today, and we talked about what I write about here. About sitting up all night in our Chiefs' arbor, sitting there between him and the second chief. Talking in quiet voices. Watching our dance. Keeping our eyes on the fire, our Grandfather, Di-Ch'o. Us talking about what we have, what it means. Talking about how few people we have keeping this going. We appreciate the members who show up for our main day—living away and returning for those one or two days in July. But there is so much work carried on by just a few in the weeks and months to get us to that one day in July. That Green Corn Day, the core of our traditional ancient ceremonies. We have no other choice. We know no other way. We do what we have to do, what we were shown. Chief agreed, he understood. He said people need to know holding our old ones is wrong. To know why it is wrong.

That was our third dance of our ceremonial cycle, leading to our Green Corn. Other tribes stomp dance, too. Our friends the Muscogees, the Cherokees, the Shawnees, they have the same (or similar) religion, similar ways. They also have few carrying on this way of life. Some other tribes, other Indians, also stomp dance, but for them it is social. Maybe at their pow-wows, during the day, exhibitions at schools, for an hour or two in the evening. That, though, is not us. Ours is religious, ceremony, sacred, spiritual. We dance all night, till sunup. Around our medicine fire. Others have no idea this Euchee world exists. What it takes to carry it forward. What it means. How it can slip away, like it has for thirty of the forty-four ceremonial grounds of the Muscogee Nation that arrived in Indian Territory with us in the 1830s. Gone. Fires extinguished. No more medicines. We Polecats remain one of the thirteen or fourteen active grounds within the Muscogee Nation. My old chiefs said it's *hard* being Euchee, *hard* being Indian. We don't do things the easy way.

Seven thousand Dzogala.

My old chief Jim, now gone for over twenty years, a full-blood Euchee, a fluent Euchee speaker, sat in our chief's seat for years and years. His dad, long gone by the 1980s, had been an Indian doctor. What you call a medicine man. Jim's dad was the real thing, not one of these pretend ones. He knew *three or four hundred* healing songs and the medicines that went with them. A highly Indigenous-educated man. Sonny, Jim's son, sat in the main chief's seat for some ten years after Jim passed. I really liked Sonny, helped him however I could as he carried out his duties. In helping Sonny during those years, I began to understand how much work it takes to carry this forward. Sonny said the only time he remembered seeing his grandpa get really mad was when people talked about doing our dances out in public, socially. His grandfather believed there was one place to do them, and if people wanted to dance, they had that place. At our grounds. Now, though, we have many members who go to indoor dances, social dances. That is their choice. Whatever people may do out there, Polecat is still the real thing. These things we still have are sacred. Our friends the Muscogee believe this, too. When I worked with their traditional chiefs to translate the *United Nations Declaration on the Rights of Indigenous Peoples* (*Declaration*) into their Mvskoke language, they understood. They heard their Old People explain in their language long before the *Declaration* was adopted the substance of what Article 31 addresses:

Hiyomakat pum ayetv pum wihokat vcacvket omet sahkopanetvt okot omes.

(Now this is our ways that was given to us and is very sacred and is not to play with.)

In remarkably plain language, that is the meaning of the *Declaration*'s Article 31.

Seven thousand Ancestors.

In boxes, on shelves at Harvard.

Let that sink in.

We have four chiefs at our stomp grounds. As far as I know, we are the only one like that. All the other stomp grounds have two chiefs. But we are a big grounds, there is a lot to being the main ground for the Euchee—the only place certain things can be done to continue us as Euchee people.

About 4:00 A.M. that last Saturday morning our stickman picked Chief to lead. I call Paige, our current main chief, a young man, but he's in his midforties now. Our old chief, Jim, my chief when I started coming around in the late '70s, put him in the fourth chief's spot. Paige was thirteen at the time. Jim sat that young boy down next to him and said:

"*You're done playing. It's time to sit here. Beside me. Time for you to watch. To listen.*" After that, there at our grounds, our young chief didn't get to go and play like the other boys. That boy didn't know then the day would come when he would have to sit in the old man's spot. Jim told him it would. And it did come. It has come for all of us. Thirty years have passed since that boy became a chief. As many years as NAGPRA has been law. Harvard has had thirty years to become a leader, to learn to do the right thing, to stop playing.

After Chief led last Saturday—Sunday morning actually—we sat down again in the Chiefs' arbor. One of our other older members, about my age, came over and shook Chief's hand and thanked him. He said he wanted to talk to him. He told Chief our old chief would have been proud. Chief's grandfather would have been proud. That those old men, now all gone, would be proud. He knew this because that member said he saw Jim and two others out there, watching Chief lead. You could hear the emotion in his voice as he spoke to Chief. He said, "I just wanted you to know." With that, he shook Chief's and my hand and went back to the north warriors' arbor.

That struck me. I was second behind Chief as he led that dance. I had been thinking about Jim while Chief led. Thought about how Jim used to lead. I thought about how the couple of main chiefs we'd had since Jim didn't lead stomp dance. Those couple of chiefs knew more than I ever will about our ceremonies and dances. They were good men. They just did not lead, didn't sing stomp dance. Not sure why, but they didn't. I thought how good it felt to have a chief we could follow out to the fire, to lead us. I was proud of that. Indians need chiefs, real chiefs.

Seven thousand Ancestors.

In our ceremonial life, we have duties. Patience is a lesson learned every time we try to hurry things up at our grounds. Yet it is also true that things must be done on time, at their proper time. We are not allowed to wait on all things. Once we rebuild our arbors for Arbor Dance, we must have Green Corn eight days later. We are obligated. Those Spirits expect us, they have a right to those dances, a right to those medicines, to those things we do: tobacco, feasts, songs. They have a right for us to fulfill our word that we will hold medicine dance in eight days. No excuses. Those Spirits, our Ancestors, the medicines expect us to fulfill our duties to them. They await us.

Our people have died for these things, for our ways. We brought our fireplace, Grandfather, with us from Georgia in the 1830s. We were forcibly removed at gun point, yet we literally carried our fireplace with us. I don't know how they did it, but they did. I imagine other tribes have similar stories. If one would listen. We are lucky, we are still here. We still exist. They still exist.

Seven thousand Ancestors.

Locked in their own wooden reservation made of boxes on shelves in a museum at Harvard. Their own Spirit boarding schools. Separated from their people. Separated from their fireplaces, from their Grand-fathers or Grandmothers. Those places and Spirits all waiting for these Ancestors to return. Will you ask us to wait? To wait again? Ask us for our *patience*? Tell me, why should we wait? Why should we be patient?

Seven thousand Dzogala.

When just before dusk, when we need to light Di-Ch'o, our Grand-father Fire, for us to start our dance, do I tell Grandfather to be patient? To wait till I am ready?

When the Thunders come through in the middle of the night. When they bring the rains and their medicines for us. When they come look-ing for their offering, our prayers. Can I tell them, "Be patient, wait till morning when I can see. When I am not comfortable in bed." No. I think I will not be patient.

I am sick of waiting. I am tired of being patient. Waiting for your com-mittees. Of waiting for our learned friends who are working on some-thing. I am taught when one has spiritual obligations, one must comply. This traditional law has two components you do not understand:

We have obligations.

The Ancestors have rights.

Perhaps some of you holding our Ancestors are too far removed from us who sit under these arbors at night, from the women in their chairs in the dark or cooking around the campfires in the summer heat. Even our little ones fight to stay awake through the night so they may greet the sun in the morning. To see Grandpa Fire in the morning burned down to only white ashes. His white ashes like an old man's hair spread in a circle, showing his contentment with our effort. That we did what we were supposed to do. We remembered our songs, our dances, those ones gone on—our Ancestors. We took care of them. And they will take care of us. That is the compact. Our agreement. That is traditional law, our jurisprudence.

You ask us to break this compact and wait?

When we have cases in your white man courts, the judge orders us to a meeting. He tells us to show up with people with authority to make decisions, authority to settle. With the power to end the lawsuit. Which of you holding our seven thousand relations has that authority? Which of you can say yes, take your relations. Who can tell me what are you will-ing to do? Tell me, now, what is the most you are willing do? You, Har-vard, violated our people, our ways, our laws. What is too much to ask of you? I ask this on behalf of our relations. On behalf of them.

Seven thousand Dzogala.

Are you waiting till we have no one left to light our fires? No one to sing our songs, no one to sit next to our old chiefs? No one left to tell how to do these things?

The Euchee are blessed to have three ceremonial grounds with our fireplaces. Our fires are still alive. Some fifteen years ago we were asked about reburial of some Ancestors in Georgia. The three Euchee grounds' leadership, the chiefs and committee members, met together to discuss this. We talked, listened to one another, about all the things we knew about, what we were taught or heard. We talked about those old ones, our Ancestors. Our obligations to them. We decided how we would respond. How those Ancestors needed to be handled. It was not the way some other tribes would do it, but that was okay. Someone asked us, and we told them. But they asked. Asked those who might know.

I do not know if you understand this. My elders say that to learn our ways you must participate. Your people, these Harvard professors and committees, have not learned this about us. I write from a Euchee perspective, but many of my friends' tribes believe the same. You, or your Ancestors, thought you could learn about us by putting my Ancestors in a box, by studying that box. That is wrong. It was wrong then. It is wrong now. It is time for you to learn. It is time for those who might have known this to remember what is right. What you are doing is still wrong.

We were stolen. Imprisoned. Hidden.

You have studied us, formed committees. You hide in academic shadows and papers. Patience? I think not. That time has gone. We wait to know you returned them home. But do not ask for my patience.

Seven thousand Ancestors.
Sixteen thousand digadi.
Dzogala, Wafuhnji-jehn?

Part 2

RABBIT AND JACKSON

Rabbit and Turkeys

I recorded this story by Ida (Clinton) Riley in the early 1990s at a nursing home in Bristow, Oklahoma, when Ida was in her nineties. This is what we call a di'ile, a traditional story that usually involves animals, sometimes with a moral, sometimes simply a story. Rabbit was often the protagonist but was not always involved. At the time I recorded these stories, I was coordinating our Euchee-language class in Sapulpa, with the participation of many of our remaining fluent Euchee speakers. The speakers loved these di'ile, often not having heard them for many years, and loved working on the English trans-lation. The Euchee writing used here is the form the elder Euchee women of the class preferred at that time, though as noted in the intro-duction, the current Euchee-language programs use a different alpha-bet for their students. Most of the other stories use a slightly updated version of those Euchee women's Euchee alphabet. However, this form is slightly easier to read for nonlearners, if perhaps not as exact.

Shaw-jwaw-na baw doo-a s'ah-baw yah-dah wa-be-thlo.
   A Rabbit was in a sack rolling down a hill.
   Daw-ka wa-g'ah-chaw-chaw.
   Just a-laughing.
Wa-chaw-ah ga-wa-ge-jehn-faw. Shaw-jwaw-nuhn-nuh wa-g'ah-gah yun-jwah.
   Turkeys were going by. They heard Rabbit laughing.

51

S'ah-baw da-daw-ha aw-yun-gah.

They came to the edge of the hill.

Shaw-jwaw-na wa-nuh gaw-law k'ah-thlah-ahn wa-thlaw ge-wa'na.

To see what Rabbit was doing.

Wa-chaw-ah wa-nuh Shaw-jwaw-na wa'na. Wa-de-da-suh wa-yu-neh-neh wa-tah dahn-che yon-ah-na.

Rabbit saw the turkeys. He asked them if they would like to try.

Baw de-la wa-thlaw.

He got back in the sack.

Da-puh-la yah-dah wa-be-thlo.

And rolled down the hill again.

Da-puh-la wa-chah-ah wa-nuh yo-ahn-na wa-yu-neh-neh wa-tah dahn-che.

He asked the turkeys again if they wanted to try.

Ga-ahn-wa-thlaw da-lahn wa-gwaw he-t'a-la hah ga-ahn wa-thlaw-dahn.

They said they would, except one.

G'ah-shtaw-ahn-da wa-gyon-na g'o-yu-thlah.

Finally he changed his mind.

Baw che de-wa-thlaw.

And got in the sack.

Shaw-jwaw-na baw-che yuhn-kwah hahn-da suh-haw-la nawn-haw-ahn yah-dah yuhn-be-thlo.

The Rabbit tied it up and he rolled it down the hill once or twice.

Baw-che wa-de-d'ahn daw-wa-paw hahn-da ga-la wa-g'uhn-thlaw.

Then he threw the sack over his shoulder and carried it home.

Baw-che do-daw-ha de-yuhn-dahn hahn-da wa-g'aw-don-nuh neh-ko-yuhn-taw yuhn-gwaw.

He put the sack in the (corn) crib and told his wife not to open it.

Wa-g'aw-don-nuh o-gwaw "we-gah-baw-de-wa-haw."

Or:

Wa-g'aw-don-nuh o-gwaw "we-gah-baw-de-che goo-yu."

His wife said, "I wonder what he has inside?"

Do-daw u-daw-sh'e ko-yuhn-taw. "De-na" wa-gwaw.

Or:

De-na seo-gwaw do-daw u-daw-sh'e ko-seo-taw.

"I am going to see." She opened the crib door.

Ko-seo-taw-ha wa-chaw-ah wa-nuh he-la ga-wa-stuh-nuh.

When she did, all the turkeys scattered.

He-t'a-la wa-da-ha seo-huhn-lahn.

She managed to catch one by the leg.

"Go-da-neh do-huhn-lahn" seh-gwaw.

Or:

"Wa-da-a-la do-huhn-lahn" seh-gwaw.

She said, "I caught a leg."

Shaw-jwaw-na o-gwaw "E-daw-she-faw neh-ko-yuhn-taw waw-suh-gwaw-jehn. Neh go-da-a-la do-huhn-lahn hahn-gwaw."

Rabbit said, "Don't just say you caught a leg, I told you not to open the door."

"Dza-shaw-he g'uhn. Wa-chah-ah oh-nuh wa-uhn-t'waw hahn-da wa-uhn-thlah."

"Make some hot water. We will kill the turkey and eat it."

De-g'aw-de neh ha-nuh guh'aw huh-uhn-zo-thlah dahn-che huhn-do-ahn-neh-jehn.

"I have asked my friends to eat with us."

Nah-hah thle-ha thlaw-ha wa-shaw yo-sh'ehn hon-da-aw-behn-wuh.

"They are bashful. When they get here, you have to wait outside."

Yaw-staw-daw-go-thlah-na-che shahn-shahn sa-thlaw. Hahn-da thlaw-ha seo-thlaw jehn.

She set the table. Then she went outside.

Shaw-jwaw-noon-nuh wa'wa-da yaw-staw-daw-go-thlah-na-che yu'la-o-da daw-ga jah-jah-hahn wa-nuh.

Rabbit was talking and walking around the table making noise.

Daw-daw-na he-t'ahn-ga de-wa-thlah, wa-sh'ahn-haw gaw-la-wa-g'wahn da-shahn-ahn.

Or:

Daw-daw-na he-t'a-t'a-shtaw-doo-thlah, wa-sh'ahn-haw gaw-la-wa-g'wahn da-shahn-ahn.

He ate out of each plate, piling the bones beside them.

Geh-da u-de-guh-nuh hon-fa-da han-hon-gwaw.

He told her, "They are gone now, you can come in."

"Wa-chah-ah wa-nuh he-la hon-law-haw wa-sh'ahn haw-la ho-wah."

"They ate up the turkey, all that is left is the bones."

"Wa-sh'ahn haw-la-da neh dza yo-doo-doo ha-de-guh."

"Just suck the soup [juice] off the bones."

Jackson and the Old Man

These days, our Old People, the Spirits, must get lonely for us who believe in them. Their land and places are no longer filled with tribal peoples, now nothing more than concrete and nonbelief, with empty otherness. Thinking of what this means for them, and us, one can imagine dialogues between one who lives quietly within this almost world and the Spirits whom we are tied to, Spirits that are tied to us. Our ceremonies are filled with stories of how things came to be, of how they are to be done, or simply of how our things are. Maybe through new stories we can understand how we view our sacred sites, Indigenous rights (perhaps more accurately Euchee rights) in a non-Western context. How differences in perception mean differences in legal duties. Perhaps the following explains some of these ideas, or perhaps the following is just a story. Perhaps a character like Jackson puts together those qualities we saw in many of our Old Euchee People. Or, perhaps, Jackson represents those things we wish we were.

L ately, Jackson had been thinking of old things. Remembering Old People who had gone on and the lands tied to those elders, the history they told of places and people. He thought about how there were fewer places left that still felt of his people. Those old ones were a hard people. Not mean or uncaring, but hard as in survivors, carrying on when people today would break. Nowadays, Jackson had to travel farther and farther to find these fewer and fewer places. Land that still showed memories. His grandparents' old place used to be in the country, but now big houses surrounded the old allotment, built by *gaga-wenuh*, white people, trying to escape the city. The *gaga* built so many houses out there that now it was the city. His mom grew up in these areas before all the non-Indians moved in. His mom always said *gaga*, and really, she was right. Hardly anyone else could afford those houses. It seemed that anywhere Euchee had been, it was always *gaga* that were going to take over their old lands. Nobody ever moved Indians so Blacks, or Asians, or Hispanics could have their land, Jackson thought to himself. His mom, born a decade after Oklahoma became a state in 1906, grew up speaking her language even when others gave it up because of the boarding schools. His mom's people were stubborn. Like Jackson said, a tough people. Those old ones must have been stubborn, or maybe just mean, he laughed, us being such a small tribe but still having our language and ceremonies.

A few years before his mom passed, she asked Jackson to take her to some of those old homesteads, the cemeteries, and the other places. Sitting in the truck looking out the window as he drove, she talked about how her dad, Jackson's grandpa, would hitch the horses to the wagon while her mom gathered supplies and things. Then her mom and dad loaded her, her brothers, and sisters in the wagon and headed down to Grandmother's. She said it was the better part of a day trip in the wagon. Jackson imagined his mom, uncles, and aunts playing in the back as Grampa drove the wagon. Of course, now it was only a twenty- or thirty-minute drive in his truck, at seventy miles an hour, rushing past the houses and businesses, all the concrete, brick, and tin buildings along the highway.

Mom would just shake her head, telling Jackson how her dad used to say before she was born, when Grandpa was a boy, they used to have a stomp ground just down from her grandmother's place. Now that could never happen, too many people, too loud, too many complaints, too many people looking on, no space.

"All those white people certainly would not like all those Indians! Not to mention the open fires," his mom would say, shaking her head and making a *tsking* noise. "Those days are gone. I feel sorry for the land, all covered up. I bet it can't even breathe. This place must miss us," she would say. Then she got quiet thinking about the places and family that were no more. "There used to be an old cemetery down a dirt road, next to the stream. I remember a little grave there. That was where they buried my aunt's baby," she said as she pointed toward a paved road with a "Private" sign on it.

Maybe it was because Jackson was remembering his mom and their road trips, thinking about those old places and what she had told him. Maybe that was why the Old Man showed up. Or maybe it just was. He didn't understand these things. But he didn't really worry much about them, he just accepted that it happened. It just seemed to happen to him more than he expected.

That evening was a nice night, and Jackson was sitting out back by the fire. He had a spot for it, he kept it clean, since it was an Indian fire. He used his flint rock to start it, so he could think and sometimes pray. He usually didn't drink coffee at night except when he was at a dance. Tonight, for some reason, though, he made coffee. He liked the taste, but he might enjoy more the act of drinking it, hot, warming one's insides, black and strong. He didn't like alcohol anymore, but he did drink coffee. Jackson might not sleep later, but for now the warm, steaming cup felt good in his hand. He was sitting, enjoying the solitude, the fire, the night, not thinking about anything in particular. As he sipped his coffee in the shadows across from the fire, he heard a voice ask if anyone was sitting in the other chair.

Jackson paused and looked around before answering, "*Huh'na,* I don't believe there is . . ."

The light of the fire and the shadows it cast meant Jackson couldn't see the stranger very well but sensed he was older. The stranger sat down, and they both sat enjoying the evening.

"I smelled your coffee—I used to like drinking it at dances," the visitor finally said.

"Me, too. Would you like some? I have more," Jackson answered.

"Thank you, I wish I could. I'll just enjoy you enjoying your coffee," the visitor said, Jackson feeling more than seeing the visitor's slight smile.

Jackson wasn't much of a talker, and apparently the Old Man wasn't either. Jackson finally asked if he was from around here.

"Well, I was at one time," the Old Man said.

Then they were quiet again. Jackson wasn't old, but he was old enough to realize there weren't many left now who were his elder, and Jackson could tell without seeing him that this was an old man, probably very old. Jackson realized the Old Man was talking Euchee, old Euchee, not abbreviating everything. Jackson's old friend Gob'a used to talk that way, having learned from his uncle who raised him, now long gone. Even the Old People that Jackson grew up knowing only knew Gob'a's uncle as old, probably born in the 1840s just after we arrived in Indian Territory in the 1830s. Even Jackson's mom and other relations would drop some of those old particles from the ends of words, making it all just a bit shorter. Not this Old Man sitting across the fire. He put everything in there, his words pouring out like smoke from the fire, filling every crevasse of the conversation with its scent, reminding one of the old days. All those extra pieces gave his speech a cadence, a flavor, a life. Jackson could see everything the Old Man talked about. It was full. No one talked like that anymore, like listening to an entire people.

As Jackson sat there by the fire with his coffee, talking to the stranger, he began thinking of a song he used to hear the old men at the grounds sing when he was young. He missed hearing the way those old men would lead. It was different, you could tell they were old Euchee songs, from their home grounds. Not ones they picked up from some other tribe and brought back. Those old guys were all gone, and he hadn't thought of those songs in a long time. Hadn't heard this particular one since he was a boy, maybe a teen.

"You know that song has a twin. It hasn't been sung in a long while. Songs like that, they get lonesome when they aren't sung together. They miss each other," the stranger said, looking up from the fire.

Jackson thought about that for a while. He gradually started to remember, to hear, an old song that they used to sing with his song, the twin. He started to sing it.

"Yes, that's it. Sing that next time, sing them both," the Old Man said, looking at Jackson and nodding.

Jackson agreed and sang it again. Jackson could hear the Old Man smiling, and they sat there again, quietly.

Finally, the Old Man stood up saying, "*Sahnle-gaya dzoda*, Jackson. *Gehde gehlehnji* (I better go.)"

Jackson stood up and asked, "Do you mind if I ask a question?"

The Old Man paused and nodded.

"Do you, or the others, get lonely? I mean, there are fewer and fewer of us here doing what we used to do, and some of us worry about that," Jackson asked, "What happens then?"

"*Huhn*. Yes, we do," the Old Man said, standing there for what seemed a long time but was only a moment. Then, looking at Jackson, he responded, "We think about you. And we pray for you. There are fewer of you, and fewer of you who are joining us. But we, you and us, can only do what we are supposed to. Light your fire, do the best that you know how. Sing both of those songs next time. And thank you for the coffee. Maybe we will visit again." And with that the Old Man was gone.

Jackson's Little Friend

J ackson had not talked to the Old Man for a while, and he began to wonder what had happened to him, as it had been several weeks since they visited. Maybe that night was just one of those moments, the odd occurrence that sometimes happens, like when his uncle talked about when he was young and hearing Spirits heading to the grounds. Maybe because he'd been thinking about those things is why Jackson woke up in the morning and recalled, not a dream but more of a memory, listening to the Old Man telling him that night to bring coffee, in a small cup. Jackson wondered about what the Old Man had said, or thought he had said, about not drinking coffee. Guess maybe he just wanted to smell it. But what did he know about such things? It's not as if Jackson had read the Spirit handbook lately. That evening he found a small blue stoneware cup he had been given while attending a friend's ceremonies up north. He had put it up, not used it till now. He brought out the cup with his thermos of coffee, filling the cup about three-quarters full and putting it on the rock across the fire from his seat. Then Jackson sat and drank his coffee. He had enough for two or three cups, which he drank. He never felt or heard the Old Man and decided he would head back inside. He went to get the little cup and then decided to leave it. He would get it in the morning.

The next morning, he remembered the cup and went to retrieve it. The cup was where he had left it. Jackson was busy the next few days and didn't think about it or have time to sit by the fire. The fourth day, he had business in town that killed most of the day, especially when he ran into his nephew. When he finally got home and finished dinner, he remembered, again, that he should take coffee down to the fireplace. He sat and drank his coffee and left the little cup of coffee when he was done, but this time he also left a cigarette by the cup.

The next evening, just before dusk, he went down there again with more coffee. The cigarette was gone, and the cup was empty, so he filled it and sat down. It was another beautiful evening with the tree frogs seeming especially happy.

"Thank you for the coffee. And tobacco," he felt a small voice say.

"*Huhn, Neh-gala, sahnle* (It was nothing. It's good)," Jackson responded and continued drinking his coffee.

"The Old Man said you were helpful and that I might enjoy visiting with you," the voice said eventually.

Jackson nodded and laughed, saying, "Well, I don't have much else to do, and I enjoy the company."

"There aren't many around here who bother, who sit still enough to hear," the little voice in the dark answered. "Though, to be honest, there aren't many of us left either."

Jackson thought about that for a while, then asked, "Why is that? I mean, what happened to you?"

His visitor did not answer, and Jackson didn't think he was going to.

"We, us little ones, really aren't that different from you," the voice said finally. "We have our ways, our places. You and me, we are tied together." His little visitor explained how what happens to Jackson and his people happens to the visitor's people, just in what one would call a spiritual way.

"You live mostly in the physical world, and you, a few, sometimes move in the spiritual world—our world," the little visitor explained. He continued saying how, like tonight, sometimes his people moved in Jackson's world, really always moved in it, it was just that most people never noticed. Most seemed only aware when they went someplace they shouldn't or bothered things they should leave alone. He finished by saying, "The more you move away from our world, the less we get to move in your world in a way that you see us. When our places are destroyed, or desecrated, well . . ."

Jackson thought about that, and for some reason *The Hobbit* popped into his mind, when Gandalf, the elves, and Bilbo sailed off into the West, leaving the hobbits behind.

"I guess it is kind of like that," his new friend laughed. "I never thought of it that way before."

"You read *The Hobbit*?" Jackson asked, looking up.

"No, not really," his little friend said. "Kind of hard to find books our size, but I saw the movie at the drive-in before they closed that down. I liked it."

At that Jackson and his new friend both started laughing. It took them a bit to be able to talk again, Jackson being the first to speak. "Well, that, as I said, was not in my How to Be Traditional manual."

"Yes, well, we all have to do something as things change," his little friend responded. "Besides, we get lonely, too. We see less of your people, less of our own. So many of our relations and things that we know have disappeared. They are no longer here. The places we know are gone, so many of the places we were tied to are built over and destroyed. Others had the things they are tied to taken, had their ties to the world destroyed. When your people stop doing things that feed us, or others do things that they are not supposed to, pretending they know or trying to insert themselves into the relationship between you and us, what do you think happens? When they take the things that are ours, and yours? Nothing good for us."

Jackson nodded at that. By then it was late, and Jackson had an early morning ahead of him. His friend sensed this, and told him, "It's okay, we can visit more later. Just bring coffee if you would. And maybe tobacco."

Jackson said, "*Huhn*," and went back to his house.

He thought about his new friend the next few days, turning the visit over in his mind, thinking about the stories his mom and other elders would tell. Most seemed just talk of how someone claimed they saw something or felt something was around. For some of the Old People, though, like his mom and her sisters, these things were simply a part of their lives, they knew no other way. Asking them if they believed in them would be like asking them if they believed in the sun or the rain, or if their father or mother were real.

His mom was a church person, but her grandma and grandpa followed the old ways and made sure their grandkids knew those ways and grew up following them. Mom always said that Golaha was strict, and if she told them they were going to do something, they did it. Jackson had asked her what happened if they didn't do what she told them, and his mom went, "Oh . . . We never ever tried to find out. We just did it." Jackson thought that wasn't the way it was today.

If other people asked about that other, older world, those old women would just go, "Hmm . . . ," and shake their heads and not say anything, especially if they were speaking English. Among themselves, they always spoke Indian and would talk and talk. They would look at Jackson and tell him they were just visiting and laugh and start talking again. Jackson always laughed, too; he understood most of what they said, and could answer if he had to. Those elders always explained when asked about it that our ways made more sense in Indian, things were lifeless in English. Regardless, his elders spoke about such things in spiritual terms. But then, Jackson's Old People said we were all spiritual beings, so that didn't help him understand any better about his little visitor. Or maybe it explained everything. Maybe he would understand better next time, or at least someday. If there was a next time. He would try to pay more attention from here on to the small things his mother had told him that he should do; tobacco, prayers, coffee—and, he laughed, maybe even put up a little outdoor movie screen.

Decolonizing the Spirit World

Several days passed before Jackson was able to sit by his fire again. He was thinking maybe his visitor wouldn't show up or that perhaps he wouldn't see the visitor. After all, how many times does one get to hang out, visit, and drink coffee with Spirits? Still, he remembered coffee and cigarettes. He put the little cup on the far side, on top of the rock. Then he sat there watching his fire and thinking of his mom and her stories, about where she grew up, and how sad she was when she talked about changes to that area, now so built over.

"We used to have ceremonies over there, too, you know," he heard his little visitor say. "I used to go and visit, but the last time was a long time ago. My relations lived there. I'm not sure what happened to them."

Jackson thought again how different it was now from when his mom used to stay down there with her grandmother.

"Everything is changed," his visitor agreed, "all those houses and businesses. There is no outdoors left. Our streams are bricked in, the wells and springs dry or dead. We know why you can't find your medicines. We are going the same way as the river Spirits and fairies of the world those people left behind to cross the big water to come here."

Jackson paused to think about what his visitor had just said. He began to wonder what his new friend knew about those Old World fairies, well, European really, because we're old, too. It seemed such an odd thing, but it also made sense. After all, other Native peoples around the world must have been like his own people, right? And if people are similar, then what of those Spirits and beings like his friend here? So, he asked.

63

His friend responded, "Well, your people used to visit others, and help other tribes with their dances, as far back as you know, right?"

Jackson nodded, "Yes, I guess so."

"And that might take your people far away for long periods?"

Jackson nodded again, agreeing.

"Well, the same with us," the little visitor continued, "except we visited in our world. But just as here, it seems most of those places, those things, have gone away, too. I don't know, maybe they were no longer fed, either. I don't know. I haven't seen or heard from most of them in a long time."

Jackson thought about that for a while. It reminded him how sad his mom was to see those places go away. How she always put a little something out, maybe a bit of food, maybe tobacco. He never asked his mom why, but he thought he knew. Maybe he should have asked her more about why she did those things. Though Jackson could see her response to his question, a little shrug of her shoulders and a lift her hands, palms turned upward. As if to say "That is just the way it is" and "Why not?" at the same time, leaving it up to Jackson to figure it out.

"We are tied together," his friend continued, "those things that happen to you happen to us. Our Spirit world has been—what's the word some of you like to use—'colonized'?" the little visitor laughed, and said it again, "Yes, that's it. Colonized!"

Jackson noted he used the English word, and how his new friend sounded very proud of himself, showing off his knowledge. Then Jackson felt bad for thinking that about his new friend. Jackson wondered, maybe they really weren't so different.

"Our world, our people, destroyed, sold," his visitor went on, "worse, no longer believed in. And now, not even known. Thankfully, some few of you still sit, still bring coffee, still listen, and tell our stories. Just doing what you should. The Old Man was telling me about your visits. It is good to have friends, Jackson."

Jackson wondered if the Indigenous Spirit world really did need to be decolonized? He wondered what that even meant? And, thinking of some of the people he knew, what could *possibly* go wrong with that? Remembering how Rabbit claimed to decolonize the forest, Jackson shook his head and laughed. He did admit it seemed his world, physical, spiritual, or both, had been overrun by the West. He never liked how our stories were retold by white people for their own amusement or to make money, killing the sacred even while they claimed they were somehow honoring our ways. He thought white people no more honored our Spirits than sports mascots honored Indigenous people. The one satisfaction Jackson took, even though he wasn't supposed to wish ill upon others, was that the West ignored its own sacred spots. So many white men seemed intent upon raising false Spirits even for their own people, like lighting a fake medicine fire. Jackson thought about how some of them attempted to vest sacredness into false idols, like the statues of the defeated Confederate Army that was born in slavery and violence. Jackson could almost hear this Spirit world quietly asking from the shadows, "What of us? Will we be free from colonization?"

Jackson thought about what his visitor had said, how those places that gave life to his visitor and his kind were being eliminated—not purposely to kill Spirits, but nonetheless that was the effect. He wondered if that was why he was now getting so many "visitors"? He remembered a professor writing that "settler colonialism is inherently eliminatory but not invariably genocidal."[1] Suddenly, listening to his little friend, spiritual genocide became real. He looked at the places his mom talked about and how they disappeared and what was taken when those places disappeared. Perhaps the spiritual world was destroyed, too, when the Spirits tied to places and things were destroyed. Jackson's old men had told him that he needed to use his language for the Spirit world—this did not seem so different. He was not sure he could comprehend all this. His old uncle must have understood this when he talked about the physical and spiritual being one, all those years ago. Maybe they needed to be freed just as his people had to undo the grievances of the past. Jackson shook his head, thinking about it.

"That is probably all true," his friend said, looking at Jackson, "but maybe you can just continue following your ways. Maybe get a few others to learn and follow. Maybe drink some coffee by the fire. That would be good."

"I can do that," Jackson felt some relief at that, responding, "though there are fewer and fewer of us. But I will try. I can't imagine doing anything else." With that, his little friend seemed to smile, told Jackson, "*Sahnle gaya dzoda*," and was gone.

Shajwane and Gojithlah
(Rabbit and Monster)

I originally published the following traditional di'ile *in the* American Indian Law Review, *in an article titled "Traditional Juris-prudence and Protection of Our Society: A Jurisgenerative Tail,"[2] as the centerpiece illustrating how simple structures explain so much about Euchee society, if properly understood. How this little* di'ile, *what some might call a children's story, shows that society addresses problems through council meetings, discusses what is expected of its males, the results of transgressions against society, the nature of pun-ishment, and what the concept of friends and relations demands. Because this one simple story derives from and is imbued with the nature of Euchee society, there are many things we can learn from it about how Euchee people are supposed to act.*

Yet ultimately this is just a story that Euchee women used to tell their children.

A long time ago, when the Old People used to be here, they used to tell this story. That was when all the animals still spoke Euchee. (And they all spoke Euchee because they were wise animals in those days.) The animals were all gathered together to dis-cuss a problem. It seems Gojithlah (Monster) had been roaming about eating all the animals. So, they met in council to discuss how some-thing had to be done. They each looked to see who might go forth and take care of (kill) Gojithlah. Dathla (Wolf) wasn't willing. Sage (Bear)

just hung his head and said nothing. Sha (Snake) was worried he would be eaten. Shajwane (Rabbit), meanwhile, was flirting with the girl sitting next to him.

"All those others are so scared. Isn't anyone brave enough to save us from that monster?" Shajwane heard the girl ask.

"I'll do it! I'll do it if you just make my lunch for the journey," Shajwane said, wanting to impress the girl. He jumped up, "I'll take care of Gojithlah."

They were all so excited that they patted him on the back and congratulated him. Shajwane felt very proud of himself. Bright and early the next morning, the animals got up and fixed Rabbit's lunch for the trip and gave it to him. He threw it over his shoulder, and down the road he went.

As Shajwane went down the path, he began to shake as he got more and more scared thinking about what he had gotten himself into. Gojithlah was very big, and Shajwane did not want to be eaten. He would rather be flirting with the girls. Pretty soon, though, he saw Gojithlah coming down the path toward him.

"*Digadi! Digadi!* (My friend! My friend!) *Dzogala! Dzogala!* (My cousin! My cousin!) How are you?" Rabbit yelled out.

"Brother Rabbit, how are you today?" Gojithlah said, looking at him.

"Good, good, nothing's wrong," Rabbit told Monster, "Sit, sit, let's visit awhile, I haven't seen you in a long time."

They then sat and visited. They talked, and pretty soon it was getting late, and they were getting hungry. They decided to eat their lunch. Rabbit opened his lunch; all he had was some carrots, celery, and such. Monster opened his lunch and asked Rabbit if he wanted to share, but Shajwane saw a foot in there for Gojithlah's lunch. When Shajwane saw that, he started getting a little sick and told him no, he did not want any.

After they finished eating, they visited longer, and soon it was getting late.

"It's almost dark," Shajwane said. "Why don't we dance awhile?"

Gojithlah said that would be good, so they started a fire. They were about to get started when Rabbit asked Monster, "I am just curious, *digadi*, we don't get to visit much, what's it take to hurt you? I bet there isn't anything that can kill you, you're so big and strong."

"Well, you know, if you chop off my big toe, that would be the end of me," Gojithlah said. Gojithlah looked at Rabbit and asked him, "What about you?"

Rabbit looked down, saw a little bug going by, and said, "Well, if somebody were to smash this little bug, it would be all over for me."

Gojithlah looked at Rabbit and stepped away. They started dancing around the fire, having a good time. One would lead, and the other followed. Then the other would lead for a while, and the other would follow. After a while, Gojithlah was really leading. He had his head thrown back, singing. Rabbit grabbed his hatchet, and next thing you know, he chopped off that monster's toe. Monster started to jump around screaming and hollering. That scared Rabbit, and he ran off into the woods shaking with fear. Finally, he didn't hear anything, so he came back. There was Monster, dead. Shajwane took out his axe and chopped off Gojithlah's head, put it in his bag, and went back to where all the other animals were. When the animals saw Shajwane, they were all very excited. They had a big dance, a big celebration, and Rabbit got to flirt with all the girls.

That is what they used to say when they were all here.

Rabbit Decolonizes the Forest

Rabbit, whether he was to be trusted or not, often caused mischief through his antics. As noted, these stories were often told to children but not always. Sometimes they had morals to them, sometimes they seemed to recount long-ago events, and some were just stories. Regardless, Shajwane was perhaps a way to remind people of their foibles without mentioning names, thus preserving some peace among tribal relations. This story that follows, and several of the other modern tales of Rabbit, were inspired by this motif of teasing. In fact, I had written a draft of this story and read it to an academic friend and the friend's children, who proceeded to show me their latest article about decolonizing the law. I attempted, perhaps unsuccessfully, to assure them this story was not about them in particular. The footnotes are an homage to all academic writings that are so profusely footnoted, even when they, just like Shajwane, prove naught.

When they were all here,[3] the Old People told how Shajwane (Rabbit) loved his lattes. One day while Rabbit was waiting for his double half-caf no-whip latte, he overheard two girls talking about how smart Fox was. They were going on and on about how Fox's Facebook posts were so amazing, something about how he was going to help decolonize his Fox relations, his entire clan. Rabbit tried to move closer to hear why they were so excited, but he couldn't

Rabbit with latte. Illustration by Adam Youngbear.

understand what they were saying. That just made Rabbit mad. He never did like Fox, everyone was always fawning over Fox, saying he was so smart. As Rabbit waited for his latte, he decided to see what got the girls so excited. He pulled out his phone and looked at Fox's social media pages. They were full of posts about decolonizing, false narratives, and deconstructive modalities. Fox wanted "to strip away the false narrative" to return to "our origins" and send the colonizers away. Rabbit really didn't understand all the words.[4] He looked around to see if anyone was watching before he did an internet search for the terms Fox spewed so freely. As he searched the web, Rabbit got more and more worked up about everyone saying Fox was so brilliant, everyone posting how "committed" Fox was, how he led the "true animal narrative," the girls so enamored with Fox. It made Rabbit sick thinking about it.

On his way home, Rabbit kept thinking how it was "Fox this. And Fox that." It disgusted Rabbit. So much so that he couldn't even enjoy his latte. He went along getting ever more upset. After all, it was Rabbit who saved the animals that time. It was Rabbit who should be respected.[5] As Rabbit walked along, an idea came to him, a scheme to have everyone recognize Rabbit's brilliance. Then the girls would talk about him instead of that stupid Fox. Whether from his excitement or maybe just the caffeine, he began to hurry home.

The next day, Rabbit went to see his friend Bear, whom he had heard was not feeling well. When he saw Bear, Rabbit asked how he was doing.

"Well, I have not been myself lately," Bear said, "a little slow and down. I had been thinking of going to get doctored."[6]

Rabbit listened for a while and then told Bear he thought he knew Bear's problem.

"Okay," Bear said, looking at Rabbit, "What's wrong with me? What do you think is causing it, my friend?"

Rabbit stood up a little taller and said, "You are suffering from postcolonial depression."

"I haven't heard of that, postcolonial? Are you sure?"

"Oh, yes. It's kind of complicated," Rabbit said, smiling. "You need to strip away the false narrative the forest imposed upon you, and then your true nature will be freed, and you can begin healing. You should live in harmony with the forest, but it has become your master. Until you strip away the colonialist overlay from the trees, that will never happen. You will continue to suffer intergenerational depression. Once that overlay is gone, though, you will begin healing and you can return to your true bear self."

"You sure it's not that I am just eating too few berries and fish?"[7] Bear asked.

"Oh no, trust me. That is what the forest would have you believe," Rabbit said, shaking his head. "The forest is full of Schadenfreude."[8] Rabbit wasn't sure what that meant, but he knew using foreign words made him sound smarter.[9]

About that time, Wolf came wandering up. "Bear! Rabbit! My Friends! How are you?"

Bear began explaining how he hadn't felt well, but Rabbit figured out what was wrong, that it was the forest.

Wolf said, "Really? I have been feeling a bit tired, too. But I figured it was because I have been so busy chasing sheep."

"That is what the sheep and the forest want you to believe," Rabbit smiled knowingly, telling Wolf, "They have joined a postimperialist alliance to keep you in servitude. Actually, it is the forest's colonizing effect. It's pretty complicated. You probably haven't studied it like I have."

Wolf looked at Rabbit and then at Bear questioningly. Bear nodded in agreement. Rabbit was thinking how impressed those girls would be if they could hear him. Wolf asked if Rabbit could help him, too.

"Yes, I think so," Rabbit said, feeling very important. "We must strip away the false overlay and reveal the trees' true nature. Once this is done, you decolonize the forest, and you can begin to heal."

Rabbit felt excited that his plan was beginning to work. He explained that they needed to strip away all the new growth from the forest, all the bark that hid the underlying true nature, all that covered the real forest. Then they would see the reality from before.

Wolf paused for a moment, wondering to himself "from before what?" But Wolf didn't say anything because he only knew about wolf things, and Rabbit seemed so sure.

"That is going to be a lot of work," Bear said. "We are going to need help."

"It is a lot of work to set yourself free," Rabbit nodded, "but if you continue to live in a colonialist forest, you will never truly be well. You will never live like a true bear, a true wolf."

So Bear and Wolf agreed and gathered their relations and friends to begin the hard work of decolonizing the forest. Rabbit felt very important, directing all the efforts, thinking how everyone would thank him. He even had on his little beret. Finally, the work was done. Trees were bare, no leaves, no bark. None of the undergrowth. Nothing. Rabbit was very proud and told his friends.

"Now you are free of the forest," Rabbit told his friends. "You are again its master, having removed all the layers that kept you oppressed."

Of course, it did not take long for the trees to start dying. With no leaves, no berries, no acorns, the other animals and birds all left. Soon Bear and Wolf were hungry, sick, and mad at Rabbit.

Rabbit, though, just told them, "It is just because you are so colonized, so oppressed, you can't even realize you are free." And with that, he went off to get his latte with the two girls.

That is all.

The United League of Rabbits

When we were all together, we would tell of Rabbit's United League of Rabbits. That was the time when Bear noticed it had been a while since he last saw his friend Rabbit. One day, he ran into their friend Turtle, and asked if he knew where Rabbit had been, Rabbit usually being so noticeable. Turtle thought for a moment and said, "I heard he has been traveling a lot lately."

"*Huhn,*" Bear responded. "Must not be around here or we would have seen him."

"No. No, I think out East, or farther. Some kind of big gathering. Rabbit said it was very important," Turtle added.

Bear said, "Of course. Does our friend ever do something that is not big and important?" They both laughed at the truth of that.

The friends visited for a while longer, catching up on family and kids, talking about how things used to be. Bear always liked visiting Turtle; he took his time speaking, but he remembered so much about the old ways. Bear always learned something new, even if only how to look at a thing with old eyes. Finally, they parted, but as Bear was leaving, he told Turtle that if he saw Rabbit, to say hello and tell him to stop by. Turtle said he would.

The next few weeks Bear was busy. Rummaging in the forest, chasing cubs, looking in on his older aunt and uncle. Seeing friends here and there, sometimes at the ball games, sometimes just out in the forest. Though he did notice fewer of his friends seemed to be in the forest, he was more likely to see them at Walmart nowadays. It was a good

Chairman Rabbit. Illustration by Adam Youngbear.

life, one that took up a lot of time but one that kept him happy. He heard a few stories from friends about Rabbit's travels to the big cities out East, to foreign lands, too. He sometimes felt a bit envious, thinking it would be fun to see the lights, try something different, meet new animals. But that moment of envy would pass.

One day, a month or two later, when he was out for a stroll, he looked up and there was Rabbit. Bear was excited to see his friend, as Rabbit was to see Bear. After greeting each other and shaking hands, they sat to visit. Rabbit asked Bear what he had been up to. Bear looked at Rabbit and could tell from the way Rabbit was bouncing up and down that he wanted to talk about his trip. But being the good friend, Rabbit had asked first about Bear. So Bear told him his story, not that much different from what he usually did. Rabbit nodded in agreement; Bear was a creature of habit. That was one of the things Rabbit liked about him, the steadfastness, though he thought Bear should also try new things.

It didn't take too long for Bear to update Rabbit and finally ask Rabbit what he had been up to. Now Rabbit was in his element, talking about Rabbit. "You know, as Chair Rabbit of the Rabbit Clan, I have to do lots of traveling. These meetings have kept me so busy. New York, Geneva, London. It is exhausting being the Chair Rabbit, being so important. Every few weeks, every month, being asked to testify, to present, at the United League of Rabbits."

Bear looked at Rabbit and asked, "League of What?"

"Rabbits. The United League of Rabbits. It's the international organization to promote Rabbit wellness and all things Rabbit. We discuss Rabbitness, hold hearings about Rabbit aptitude, and then after lengthy discussion, we might, occasionally, enact a resolution in support of Rabbit Rights. We have great hopes that at some point we may even enter a convention that requires Rabbit Action, but that is probably years off."

Bear asked, "A convention? What is that? Isn't that what you are already doing, gathering together?"

Rabbit was very patient, his friend, after all, didn't get out much, "No, no. A convention is an agreement at the highest level where the stakeholders agree to require or prohibit an action. Our great hope is that we might someday enact a General Convention on the Rights of Rabbits to Eat Grass."

Bear thought about that, nodding his head. He was not sure he understood but told his friend that it seemed it was very important work his friend had taken up.

"Very important work," Rabbit said. "We also try to build coalitions with other animals, but that has not been as successful as we had hoped. We plan to have more hearings about how to improve on such cross-pollination efforts. We have a lot of well-known Rabbits attending that one to discuss what other animals need."

Bear, not knowing what else to say, simply said, "*Huhn.*"

Rabbit continued, "You should really attend, there are great side meetings where you could meet others interested in Animal Rights. We have the best scholars and grassroots activists."

"Grassroots activists? I thought all Rabbits ate grass roots? Aren't you all actively doing that?" Bear asked.

"Well, yes. But some of us know a lot more about eating grass than others. So, we must explain to the others, on behalf of the others, what is truly involved in grass eating. Sometimes our own Rabbits don't know what it is they are doing, they are just out there eating grass. They are lucky they have me to speak on their behalf. It is why the League was created, for animals like us to talk," Rabbit explained.

"At those unofficial meetings, we sometimes talk all night about how to be the best animal we can be, and what is keeping us from achieving our true animalness. A lot of great resolutions have come out of those late nights. I think it could make you a better Bear, my friend. Very important work."

Again, Bear just nodded. Rabbit continued, "Just seven years ago, after many years of discussions and meetings, the High Commissioner on Rabbit Rights came out with a Statement Decrying Anti-Rabbit Stories in the strongest possible terms. It was huge for us."

"I don't remember hearing anything about that. Did it help much? I still hear a lot of stories about you." Bear said.

Rabbit looked a bit mad at his friend's statement. "No, I am not sure anyone else knows about it. But it was an important moment, it has made a tremendous difference in the vocabulary we use, a game changer in the modalities by which we talk among ourselves. I have seen at least a dozen law review articles written about it."

Bear thought about it for a moment, not sure he really understood what Rabbit had just said, but told him, "That sounds like such great fun. I would love to attend sometime; you know how I love to meet others and visit. But you also know how those here depend on me for so many things, with so many family matters, ceremonies, and church doings going on now, I am not sure I have time to go learn how to be a better bear. Besides, I am not much of one for traveling. I guess I will just leave it to you Rabbit experts as to how I can be more Bearlike."

Rabbit nodded, he knew how Bear was, but he had to try. "Well, if you change your mind, let me know, I can always get you on the agenda." With that, Rabbit and Bear turned to visiting about family and friends, and how things were going in the forest, leaving the important things for discussions at a later time.

That is what we say about the United League of Rabbits.

Part 3

❧

INDIAN DOCTORS
AND DANCES

Visiting Uncle John

It is hard to know exactly how many Euchee there are today because we are enrolled within the Muscogee (Creek) Nation. There are no separate Euchee rolls, we are simply counted as Muscogee. However, we are not Muscogee. At the time of allotment in 1906, there were some eight hundred of us, at least as listed for Euchee Town on the final Creek rolls established by the Dawes Commission. We undoubtedly number more now, maybe three thousand plus, but that is just a guess. Regardless, to this day we keep our unique identity despite being surrounded and included within the much larger Muscogee people. We managed to do this even while several other distinct tribes that are related to the Creeks have all but disappeared within the Muscogee Nation. Perhaps part of the reason we remain distinct is the Muscogees could never understand our Euchee language, Euchee being totally unrelated to the Muscogees' (and everyone else's) language.

When I was in my late teens, back in the late 1970s, I started visiting my elder relations to learn more about my people. I would go to my mom's Uncle John and Aunt Acie, Jimmie and Wannie Cahwee, and Mom's other older relations, and listen to them tell stories. Some stories were about how things used to be, some about the Old People and things that happened to them. Uncle John and Aunt Acie lived south of Kellyville, Oklahoma, on John's allotment. Kellyville was a small town, with a population of about nine hundred in the 1970s, and maybe some five hundred in the 1920s and 1930s. There had always been a number of Euchee living in the area, on what was left of their allotments. I'm not sure, but I think Uncle John still had about 20 acres out there, but he didn't have his original 160 acres. I asked one of my cousins about Uncle John's land, when did he sell it, and my cousin said, "You mean have it stolen?" I don't know if it was actually stolen, but my cousin was referring to how so many Euchee lost the land they had been allotted. The Creek reservation had been cut up in the period 1898–1906 with 160 acres of the reservation allotted to each Creek (and thus Euchee) member. The vast remainder of the reservation's lands were then sold to non-Indians. After statehood in 1906, many of the lands remaining in Indian hands were quickly lost, much of it through theft, probate, or deceit, and many times these were all the same thing. The Euchee were fortunate not to have their land taken through outright murders, like the Osages, but the loss of our land base was just as real, and we all knew it and remember. So, when my cousin said stolen, I just nodded, knowing what he meant.

It was not clear to me at the time how Uncle John was related to my mom, all I knew was that my mother called them Uncle John and Aunt Acie. I think now I could explain how we were related, but that, like so many Indian relationships, would be another long, twisting story. John and Acie were both probably born sometime around 1900, just as the Muscogee Nation was cut up into allotments. They were full-blood Euchee, I think, and fluent Euchee speakers, though both could speak English, John having retired from the glass factory in Sapulpa a few years earlier. They were regular members of the Pickett Chapel, Euchee Indian Methodist Church. I am guessing they had probably joined the church sometime in the 1920s, as did my mother's family and several other Euchee. Pickett Chapel was a small church that continued to preach in Euchee through the 1960s. Our people were mostly either Indian Methodist or members of the traditional stomp grounds. Most of my mother's close relations went to Pickett Chapel, but I had heard that Uncle John used to go to stomp dances when he was young. I assume he stopped going when he started attending church. With John's deep, strong voice, he would have been a great stomp dance leader. We had other relations who continued with stomp dance, and over time, I visited them, too.

That summer I would go to visit John and Acie for a day or two, sometimes three or four, sleeping on their couch. I visited the other relations also, though I usually did not stay the night with the others. John and Acie would speak English to me, mostly. However, they only spoke Euchee to each other and on the phone, as the people they talked to were almost all Euchee; their relations and the people they had grown up with. My mother told me when I went to visit to be sure and give them something, to be polite. Uncle John loved coffee, so I would go to the store and get a pound tin of Canes coffee. He would have that coffee brewed up and gone in the few days I was there. That's probably why I didn't get much sleep at their place, as I would drink it with him, with Uncle John drinking coffee right up till bedtime. With me being new to coffee and all, I would be lying there in the dark, wide awake.

I remember their house was small, it had maybe five or six rooms, and was at the end of a short dirt driveway filled in with red-colored sandstone. John said some years back, before I came around, a couple of white men saw all that sandstone and wanted to buy a few truckloads of it to build some houses. John thought about it for a while but decided not to sell. He said the white man had taken everything else from us Euchee, so he thought maybe he would just keep his rock.

Their living room was the first room as you came in the door. In the west window, they had one of those big water coolers that people used to have before air-conditioning became common or affordable. It worked pretty well to relieve those hot Oklahoma summers, with its distinctive, almost damp feel to the air that it put out. We would sit and visit, but only after he had asked if I wanted coffee. I could hear my mom telling me to always accept what is offered, so I would say, "Okay, thank you." They would tell me to sit at the small kitchen table. John or Acie would pour a cup of coffee from the pot that was always on and then put the cup on the table in front of me. I am pretty sure that was just the first part of Aunt Acie's plan to feed me. Acie would go to the small white fridge, one of those Kenmores from Sears that everybody used to have, look in it, and ask, "Do you like *tobio dabisah* (sweet potatoes)?" I did, so she would set out a plate and fork and give me a small baked sweet potato from the fridge. Then she would say, "We have some leftover *wadza gandi* (pork chops), too," and those came out next. And, of course, if I'm eating pork chops, she had to get out some bread, because those old Euchee never ate a meal without bread. Then she would say, "Maybe I should warm up some *dzokuh dzosha* (gravy) because *dzokuh dzosha* goes with *wadza gandi* (pork chops) and *k'athlo* (bread)," using the Euchee words she thought I should know. As I had been taught to be polite, I was happy to eat whatever she set out. That's how my visits always seemed to start.

Uncle John, and occasionally Aunt Acie, would tell me about the Old People they knew, the Euchee who had gone on. When Aunt Acie thought Uncle John was misremembering someone, or forgetting something, she would speak to him in Euchee for a bit. Then she would continue in English, adding details, adding to the story he was telling. They would talk about Sapulpa in the 1920s when the downtown was full of stores. They said that on Saturday mornings in the 1920s everybody would come to town to shop, walk about, and socialize. They liked to talk about Staiger General Merchandise in Kellyville, the local store that, in the days before Walmart, carried groceries, dry goods, and most things one might need for farm or rural living. John and Acie remembered how the owner used to speak enough Euchee to sell and visit with the Euchee who came into his store.

John told how some Euchee men back in the "old days," probably the 1880s and 1890s, used to steal horses from the Indians down south or out west and drive them up north, maybe to Kansas, to sell them to the white men. Uncle John said that on the way back they would steal more horses from other white men and take them to other Indians and sell them those stolen horses, maybe to replace the ones they stole. John would say with a smile that those old Euchee were very smart. They would talk about Pickett Chapel and going to church. John told about other things that happened to those old Euchee, about the Indian doctors we used to have and about how we used to hold traditional funerals.

Both Uncle John and Jimmie Cahwee told me about the small glowing balls of light, or fire, one would see on occasion, how they were some kind of spiritual matter. Jimmie told about how one followed him home from a traditional funeral when he left too early. Jimmie's dad lived to be a very old man, into his hundreds, born sometime in the late 1860s. He had told Jimmie if he went to one of those funerals, or any other traditional things, he had to obey the rules, not leave till it was over, to behave. When he told his dad about what happened, how the light had followed him right on top of his car till it turned and disappeared through a field, his dad merely said, "I told you." Jimmie's brother William told me another story about seeing one leave the house of a very sick Euchee woman. After the light left through the front door, went down the driveway, up over the field, and disappeared, the woman got better. William believed the light was sickness leaving the woman in Spirit form.

At the time, I never thought about how such good Christian men were telling so many stories about thieves, Indian medicines, and Spirits that the Old People used to see. But these elders were proud of being Euchee, and, whether Christian or not, that is how they had grown up.

Uncle John and Aunt Acie loved their Euchee language, and that is almost the only language they spoke. The same was true for the other elder Euchee relations I visited. Because of that, by the end of the summer, without realizing it, I understood Euchee very well. Better than I do today. One Sunday morning after returning from an all-night stomp dance in Cherokee country, four or five of us stopped in to get breakfast at a small diner in Sapulpa. Georgie, an elder Euchee woman, was with us. She had gone to school with my mother and spoke Euchee fluently, like pouring water in a cup. As we sat there, my mother's cousin Jake came in and started visiting with us. Cousin Jake (Uncle Jake to me) had been a Methodist preacher when he was young, but after marrying a Baptist woman, he became a Baptist preacher. Jake also spoke Euchee extremely well and could use many of the old forms, as he was practiced in translating the Bible. In a few years, he would graciously help me learn certain things in Euchee. But, for now, Jake was asking Georgie where we had been and how we were doing. Georgie told him, and he gently teased her, kind of, that we should be going to church. Georgie laughed and answered that we had just been at church all night, Indian church. Jake just shook his head, wished us well, and went on his way. Not until later did I realize they had been speaking Euchee, and I had perfectly understood everything they said.

Euchee Doctors

Many of my older relations' stories were about how the Euchee used to have a lot of Indian doctors, especially considering we are such a small tribe. Other people, mostly whites, but even many other tribes, called them medicine men. But our people tended to call them doctors, at least in English. I like our name better because that is what they did—doctor. They treated the sick and the ill, both their physically and spiritually caused illnesses. They knew plants and how to prepare them. Each sickness had a plant. Each plant had a song. Or maybe it was a song for each illness. Maybe that is the same thing. They understood that the physical and the spiritual were tied together, in treating one you treated the other. Today, Western medicine calls that holistic medicine. To us, it was just doctoring. We don't have those doctors among our Euchee people anymore, but our traditional people still like to use plants. Herbs, as some of them call them. And we still rely on numerous medicines for our ceremonial grounds.

We were always told our Euchee doctors were powerful, respected, or feared, maybe some of each, by other Indians. Perhaps that, too, was one of the reasons we Euchee were mostly left alone and survived. Of course, not all medicines were, or are now, good. Some people used them for bad purposes, to try to harm others, or for personal reasons. But in our way of understanding, that was a risky business. Among ourselves, we will talk, quietly, about how bad medicines are "hungry." If someone sent medicine to do harm and it didn't find its target, it would return looking to feed on the one who sent it, or on someone that

84

person was close to and cared about. That's why some Euchee say that not having today some of the things we lost is not always a bad thing, some of those things needed to be put away.

Uncle John also told how owls might sometimes come around at dusk, walking or hooting. Uncle John and the others said this was a warning, maybe of sickness or perhaps of a death that had occurred. Things that were not in their proper place and time was never a good sign, like night creatures seen during the day. As some of my elders would say, some of those Old People were not good people, they may have been using bad medicine and were coming around to cause trouble. My mom's elder relations told how some could change their appearances to look like deer, owls, or other animals. That would explain why sometimes animals did not act as they were supposed to act, like maybe seeing a deer walking on its hind legs or such. The old Euchee even had a *di'ile* about animals that disguised themselves as humans to cause trouble. Mose, a brother of Jimmie, told a story about how in the 1800s some of the menfolk went hunting, maybe for buffalo—before they all disappeared. They decided to camp for the night and built a fire to cook. They were sitting there that night, and a little dog kept coming around, trying to steal some of their food. Finally, one of the men threw a stone at the dog to scare it way. The stone hit the dog, and the dog said, "Owie!" Mose said right then those men knew that dog was someone. At least that is what Mose said.

Uncle John told another story about one of his old relations who lived in the country, as did all the Euchee in the late 1800s. One evening, about dusk when the sun was setting and the shadows were long but there was still some light, he heard an owl hooting. So this Euchee knew something was up and grabbed his gun and went to investigate. Uncle John said the elder opened his door and went out on the porch and saw a big owl standing there in his yard. The man raised his gun and shot. The owl looked as if it was hit, but when the man went to look for it, he found nothing but a few feathers. Nor did he find anything the next morning. Uncle John said that a few weeks later, his relation heard that a man who lived some miles away had died of gunshot wounds. Strangely, no one had heard of any fights or disturbances. This story, with slight variations, is often told by different ones of our people. Nonetheless, this is what Uncle John said happened in the days before all the white people came.

We mostly talk about the men who were doctors, but some women doctored, too. My mother grew up with her grandmother, *golaha*, and told how people would come to her *golaha* to fix medicines when they were in need. My mother never said, and I never thought to ask, if it was men or women who asked for help. Nor did my mother say what they were needing doctored, if my mother even knew. My mother also told how her *golaha*, even though she was a church woman by then, would fix medicine every full moon for the children she was raising, which included my mother, her four siblings, and the occasional cousin of my mother. Golaha would get them all up at sunrise, herd them outside facing east, and they would all take the medicine. From what my mother said, it sounded as if the medicine was either red root or maybe snake root, like we take during Green Corn. The medicine was to purify them, clean them for the month. Her *golaha* was a good Christian woman and did not attend our ceremonial dances. Nonetheless, my mother said that growing up, she would not eat corn before the grounds had its Green Corn ceremonies and followed all the traditional medicine restrictions for women. Regardless, all those doctors, men and women, are gone now, the last ones passing away in the 1960s.

Those Old People knew a lot of things. Those elders, though, were still just people, people who had gone through very destructive times. From the pre-allotment period of the reservation in 1900, to the reservation being publicly cut up in 1906, to seeing the destruction of the tribal government and flood of white people into Euchee territory in that brief period between 1900 and 1910. Those huge changes destroyed lives, families, and tribal society. Those were hard times for our people. Changing so much of the Euchee's old ways of life. Not surprisingly, this trauma meant some Euchee ended up drinking, a lot, by the 1920s and 1930s. (And nowadays, too, for that matter.) Alcohol's pull reached my mother's mom and dad, which is why my mom's *golaha* swept up her and her siblings and raised them. I suspect that was one of the reasons many Euchee joined the church between 1906 and the 1920s. Prior to 1906, though the Christian church made inroads with other tribes such as the Muscogees, the Euchee had been resistant to conversion, sticking to our old religion at the stomp grounds. We hear stories about drinking and fights that occurred among the ceremonial people around those times. With the church preaching abstinence from alcohol, it must have been very enticing to join the church for those who did not approve of drinking and the destruction it caused. The severe changes could also have made one question the ways one had followed previously and be susceptible to new ways, to conversion. But it is worth remembering that even some of the Euchee who became church people also, or still, drank.

Back in the 1920s and '30s, those old Euchee would often drink at the beer joints in the Black part of town in Sapulpa. The Indians probably weren't allowed into the white bars or places, so they would go where they were welcome. When they had too much drink, or they were out on the streets whooping (mom called it their war cry), they would get picked up by the Sapulpa police and tossed in jail till they sobered up. Indians might not be good enough for the white bars, but they were good enough for the white jails.

I don't remember if it was Uncle John or one of my other elder relations who told me about one weekend, probably a Saturday, back in the 1920s or '30s, when several of those old Euchee were drinking and got themselves arrested. I say old, but that's because we knew them as our elders, but at the time they were probably mostly young men. They had been sitting there in the jail cell for a while when the jail door opened, and Doc Johnson got tossed in with them. He'd been picked up for drinking, too. My mom and her relations always talked about Doc Johnson being a really good Indian doctor, powerful. (Doc was his English nickname; I am sure the old Euchee used his Indian name, but I don't recall it.) Those old Euchee sat there visiting, sobering up, for an hour or two.

Finally, Doc Johnson got up and said in Euchee, "*Huhn, godate*" (Well, this is long enough). He went to the jail door, bent down to the lock, blew on it, and the door swung open a bit. Doc Johnson pushed it open and left. The other Euchee looked at one another, but they didn't want to get in more trouble. They knew the routine. They would probably be let out once they sobered up, so they didn't leave. Uncle John said that about two or three hours later the jailers opened the cell door again. And again, there was Doc Johnson. The Euchee men all teased him about getting picked up, again. After another hour passed, Doc Johnson got up and said in Euchee, "*Godate, gehde gelehnji*" (That's long enough, time to go). He bent down to the door's lock once again and blew on it. As the door swung open, Doc Johnson turned to the other Euchee and said, "*Nechi, neh-dine depuhle*" (This time, you won't be seeing me again). And he left. Doc Johnson was right: he didn't get picked up again. All the Euchee men looked at one another. They all knew why. They all knew why he wasn't going to get picked up again. They knew he flew away. The Old People said Doc Johnson was a powerful doctor. We don't have anyone like that among us anymore. Anyway, that's what my old relations told me.

I wish I could remember half the things Uncle John, Aunt Acie, and the others talked about. I was too young to know what I didn't know, or to realize what I should have asked them. I do know, and knew then, that I was lucky to sit and drink coffee and eat a little leftover sweet potato with Uncle John and Aunt Acie, and to have similar visits with other elder relations. Most of my mother's elder Euchee relations passed away by the mid- to late 1980s, and now my mother's generation is gone, too. My mother's elder relations were humble, quiet people, but like all my elder relations, when asked, they would willingly share whatever they had, whether it was a leftover sweet potato, their home, or stories.

Jackson Almost Learned
to Doctor

One Thursday morning in August, Chief called to talk about going to a dance that weekend. He was thinking about going to one of the Cherokee grounds. I said okay, that sounded good to me. We always try to follow our chief to wherever he goes to dance. Afterward, I called Jackson and told him. We decided we would caravan down Saturday afternoon; we wanted to get there early and knew Chief wouldn't go till later that night. Saturday came, and we loaded up the wives and headed out early, in time to get there for supper. We pulled in when it was still light and parked where our bunch always did. Most people, if they visit regularly at another grounds, have a place where they normally park and sit. We got our chairs out, leaving the women's shells in the vehicles, since it would be several hours before the dance started. We set up the chairs in front of our vehicles where we could see the grounds, in our usual spot. I set my chair next to Jackson, and the women set theirs a bit behind us, next to each other. We sat there just relaxing, we'd been there maybe thirty or forty minutes when a young man came over and greeted us, shaking our hands, and asked us, "*Oseo!* Where ya'll from?" We told him Polecat and introduced ourselves by our first names. He said, "That's what Chief thought. He wanted to invite you to come over and eat with him, if you're hungry."

Jackson turned to the wives and asked, "*Nehdze wahane neh-yahuhn-le?*" (You old women hungry?).

Jackson's wife responded, "*Nego'ahn wahane.* (There're no old women here). And if you want to eat when you get home, you better behave."

Jackson laughed and told the young man, "I guess we can eat." We all got up and followed the young man to the chief's camp. As usual, they fed us well there. When we finished eating, we sat and visited for a while. We were all friends with the chief there; he was always good about coming to our grounds to help us out, so we caught up on where we had gone to dance that summer, how other ceremonial people we knew were doing, and other small talk. After a bit, Jackson and I decided to go back to our chairs, but the wives stayed at the camp to visit. Jackson's wife knew the chief's wife, and they were catching up on what kids were doing what. By the time we sat in our chairs again, the sun had set, though it hadn't cooled off much. Some of the young guys would show up in shorts and change before the dance started, but we always were in jeans and boots. We might put on a long-sleeve shirt when the dance started, but for now, we were comfortable in short-sleeve shirts or T-shirts. Jackson always had that kerchief around his neck, too. Rolled up with the loose ends hanging down the front of his shirt. I think he thought it would catch the sweat. For me, when I wore it like that, it just made me hot. Up at Polecat, it was helpful in keeping the red-clay dirt out of the shirt, kind of. Not that anything stopped that dust.

It would be another couple of hours before the dance started, maybe around 11:00 P.M. Our crew—we were expecting maybe a couple more carloads—would probably come rolling in about the time the dance started. It always took them a while to get going, as they had kids, ball games, or just took their time getting around. Some might even hit the casino before they showed up. But Jackson and I liked to get there early, to sit and just be there. Our Old People used to say there was no place more beautiful than the grounds. Sitting there looking at the square grounds with its brush arbors, the camps of the families, and smelling the ever-present smoke from the grounds' fireplace. Whether it was our grounds or one of our friends' places, it was good to be there. White people might like visiting the great cathedrals in Europe, but we liked visiting stomp grounds, our cathedrals. It was always nice to get around to other stomp grounds. We didn't have ceremonial duties here, unlike at our home grounds. Here we weren't the chief, stickman, speaker, committee member, or whatever. We didn't have to sit under the arbors on those hard wooden logs that never got any softer. We could sit in our comfortable chairs with backs, some even had a little cup holder on them nowadays. We could get up and visit, or just sit and listen to the dance. We didn't have to get out and help every round (when a leader goes out to lead a dance), we could just sit and listen to them lead, if we wanted. We loved our grounds, but it was nice being a visitor.

I had been wanting to talk to Jackson about his great uncle Phillip, and tonight seemed like a good time to ask. Phillip had been one of our last, maybe *the* last, Indian doctors, medicine men, that we had. A good one. Phillip's uncle and grandfather were both doctors and had trained Phillip when he was young, before he went off to World War I. Those old doctors had to know a lot of plants, and the songs to go with them, in order to doctor people. There was a lot of knowledge in those Old People. Some women would doctor, too, but I knew less about that. As I remembered, Phillip had passed away in the late 1960s, and I wondered why Jackson had never learned medicines from his great uncle.

We sat in the dark and sipped our too-hot coffee from the Styrofoam cups. The area was dimly lit by the fireplace on the square grounds, the moon, and the few camps they had. These camps surrounded the square grounds on three sides, set back from the grounds, just across the dirt road that circled the grounds. We talked about kids and Old People we knew, and how they were related to other Old People, and to us. Finally, I asked Jackson when his uncle Phillip had passed away. Jackson said, "Maybe ten or eleven months after I got back from the service, it was less than a year, maybe late 1968?" Jackson said he was running around raising hell when his uncle Phillip passed away. Jackson went on that he continued to run around for a while after his uncle passed. But he thought about what his uncle said and started to settle down, slowly. Then he met his future wife and he started settling down, more or less, for good.

I told Jackson, "I heard he wanted to teach you how to doctor, I guess he ran out of time."

Jackson paused for a moment "Uncle did want to teach me, at one point, before I went into the service. I was twenty when I joined. Once I came back, he was going to teach me, but that changed." Jackson was staying at his mom and dad's place when he went in the service. One day, his dad's uncle Phillip stopped by to talk with Jackson. Phillip and Jackson's dad were always close. Phillip, who was in his seventies by then, always took his uncle role seriously, *dzet'ahns'e* (little father), to Jackson's dad. So Jackson was a little surprised that day when his dad poured them coffee and then went back outside. Jackson and his uncle sat there, drinking coffee for a while, not talking about much of anything, just asking about friends or relations, what the other had done lately.

Laughing about who had got drunk and in trouble. Occasionally not saying anything.

After Phillip drank most of a second cup, he started in: "You need to be at my house tomorrow morning before sunup. You're leaving for the service soon; you need to be ready for what's about to come. After I fix you up, then we can talk." With that, he got up and went outside.

Jackson's dad came back in after speaking to his uncle Phillip for a moment or two. Jackson's dad said, "Don't be late tomorrow, get there early." Jackson nodded; he knew that Uncle was talking about medicines. He also knew Phillip had been in the army in Europe during the First World War. He had joined when war was declared. When he was younger, Jackson had overheard Phillip talking about his service with other veterans, so Jackson looked up to Phillip as a veteran. I told Jackson I'd heard the same thing from my older relations about Phillip. Those old Indians had a lot of respect for Phillip, not only because of his doctoring but because of his military service.

Jackson continued, saying the next morning, he got up early and went to see his uncle. He knew not to eat or drink anything before he went. His uncle hadn't even bothered to remind him. When Jackson got there, he could tell Phillip had been up for a while and had everything ready. He talked to Jackson for a while, telling him what he might see in the service. Then Phillip told Jackson about the warrior medicine, what it would do for him.

I had heard others talk a little about this warrior doctoring, but this was the first time I'd heard the whole story. But I won't go into what Jackson said about the details. Some things need to be heard or done in person. Some things are like that, like our dances, they need personal connection. My elder relations had been that way. They were always willing to share with me, but about some things they would say, "I'll tell you this, I will show you how. But if someone else wants to know, they can come ask." I think that was because they wanted the person to show commitment, to know they would take care of what they learned. "This isn't something to play with" was how they put it.

Anyway, Jackson went on, explaining that Uncle Phillip had said what he did for Jackson wasn't a guarantee, nothing could guarantee the future. But it would protect him, show him a way forward, help take care of him if he took care of it. If he listened. I knew some of our Euchee men had been doctored before they went off to World War II. Almost all our men were fortunate to come back, only two didn't that I knew about.

When Phillip was done doctoring Jackson, they went inside Uncle Phillip's house. His wife was up and had breakfast ready. She set the table, poured some coffee, then went into the other room, leaving Jackson and Phillip to eat and talk. Phillip ate about half his plate, then paused. "You a bit old, I been watching you, and not just because you my nephew." Phillip said in that style of English those old Euchee used, mixing English and Euchee words and grammar together. Then he continued talking mostly in Euchee, which back then Jackson understood pretty well. "When you come back from the service, you need to come see me. I need to teach things; someone needs to learn how to take care of our people."

Jackson stopped his story to drink some coffee. After a bit, he continued, "I knew Uncle was talking about learning how to doctor. My dad was supposed to have learned when he came back from World War II, but Dad had run around for a while, drinking mostly," Jackson laughed, "I know, sounds familiar right? Anyway, Dad settled down, started working, and had a family, and never did learn."

I said to Jackson, "And that's where you came from . . ."

Jackson laughed and said, "Yup."

Wilson Gets a Wife, Almost

About then another car rolled up behind us. We heard the doors opening and people getting out. We could hear them talking behind us. Jackson said, "Sounds like Will is here. Hope he brought some women; we need shell shakers." I just nodded in the dark. In a couple of minutes, Will came up, carrying his chair, shining his flashlight to see. He saw us and said, "Hey, it's the old guys." Jackson and I laughed, Jackson pointed to the spot next to him, Will opened his chair, set his light down, and then shook our hands and sat down. I shined my flashlight to where our women were sitting. Will got back up and helped his wife and daughter set up their chairs. They came and shook our hands and asked where our wives were. We pointed to the chief's camp, and they started that way. One paused and asked, "I suppose you men need us to bring you coffee, don't you?" Jackson grunted and said, "I guess so, since you up there." After the women left, Will asked, "Is Chief coming?" Jackson looked at Will and said, "I thought you were chief." Will snorted and said, "You know better than that, what would I do with all that pay?" It was a running joke, as of course there was no money involved in being chief. And too much work. A lot of people thought it would be cool to be chief. We knew it was a twenty-four/seven job. One was always chief, that work came first before all else. Or it was supposed to. I told Will, "I talked to Chief on Thursday, he said he was coming." Will responded, "Hope he brings a few more leaders; with this small crowd, they might be coming to pick us every other round. . . ." We laughed in agreement, not that we would mind too much.

We sat there for a while, then I told Will, "Jackson was just talking about when he got back from the service and about his uncle Phillip. Will nodded in the dark and waited for Jackson to start in again. Will said, "I remember Grandpa Phillip." Phillip wasn't Will's blood grandfather, but he had looked out for the young boys during Green Corn, so they all, like Phillip, called him Grandpa. "I knew he was a doctor, but I remember he was a bit, umm, how would you say, earthy?"

Jackson laughed at that. "A bit. Damn. He was flat nasty sometimes. A great doctor. But he did like to tease. A lot of those old men, and women, were that way. That way nowadays, too." We all laughed; we might have been guilty of it ourselves on occasion.

Jackson started again. "You ever hear the story about Wilson? Why they called him Thlahpa[1]? Wilson had been another one of our home bunch and had been a year or two older than Jackson. Will nodded no, so Jackson continued: "He used to make turtles, good ones. Quite a few of the old women wore turtle shells he had made. When some of the women down south saw and heard his turtles, he started selling them to those women from those grounds, too. Of course, Wilson had been a boxer, and was a good-looking young man. Girls would fall all over themselves for him, especially as he was a good leader. Anyway, one weekend, maybe a year before I went into the service, Uncle Phillip loaded us all up to go to a grounds down south. Uncle Phillip was always welcomed, grounds people knew him, respected him. But we didn't take any shell shakers with us. That wasn't a problem, as they had a bunch down there. We got there and set up our chairs and one of Uncle's friends came to sit with us. After the dance started, Uncle was the first one of us they picked to lead, the Meko knew Phillip. So we all followed Uncle out, and the shell shakers jumped in to help. Turns out Wilson had made some turtles for Uncle's friend's granddaughter, a big old girl, she was maybe around twenty. She could really shake shells, loud, too, with those turtles."

Jackson paused for a sip of his coffee before continuing. "That girl had gone out when she noticed her grandfather helping Phillip and must have noticed Wilson. When Uncle Phillip ended, she followed us back to our chairs, pretending to talk to her grandfather but really trying to flirt with Wilson. It was a small crowd, so it wasn't too long before the stickman came around again. Phillip pointed at Wilson and said get him next. That girl was still there, so she jumped in behind Wilson. Wilson sounded good that night, and that girl shook her shells hard. When they came back, the girl said a couple of her turtles felt loose, could he fix them? Wilson looked at her grandfather, and he nodded that it was okay. Since Wilson had made them, he agreed. Wilson asked me to hold the flashlight so he could see. He knelt down in front of the girl, she lifted her skirt up, and he started messing around with the sinew he used to tie the turtles together and to the leather that held everything in place on a woman's legs. He was really jerking on the string, so the girl put her hand on Wilson's head to steady herself. It looked to me like she was holding him down there, kneeling before her and all. I think she might have been holding him down. It took him four or five minutes to get them turtles straightened up and fixed, all the while he was kneeling in front her, the skirt hiked up so he could see the turtles. As he knelt in front of her pulling, her hand on his head, his head was bobbing back and forth at her waist, looking like she was pulling his head back into her. We all sat there watching, me, Uncle, and the girl's grandpa."

Jackson went on that finally, Wilson got up and said, "There, that should do it."

Uncle said, "It sure should!"

Wilson looked at Uncle Phillip and said, "What?"

Uncle told Wilson, in his serious voice, "*Huhn. Gahshtale wa'aneonuh seogwajehn, nehdze henehtuya ikanle neh dze wed'ik'ada. Thlahp'e bishahn nehdze neh-g'adonnuh deguhn.*" (Well, in the old days, the old women said if you going to sniff it that long, you gotta marry it. Ten more seconds you woulda had a wife.)

The girl's grandpa looked at Uncle, knowing some Euchee, said, "*Nehdze Dzo-gala!*" (We would have been related!)

Even in the dark Wilson started looking pale, and the girl wasn't sure what to think. Then Uncle and his friend started laughing. Wilson suddenly decided he had to go relieve himself and fled into the woods. The girl stood there for a moment, then started laughing, too, and told us to thank Wilson. She asked her grandfather if it was okay, she would go sit with her friends now. But if Wilson wanted to talk, to come look her up. With that, she left. Wilson finally reappeared after an hour but didn't go out to dance the rest of the night. As we were loading up in the morning to head home, Uncle Phillip asked Wilson if he needed to talk to his wife before we left. Wilson just answered, "No."

"After that night we all started calling Wilson 'Thlahpa' (Ten). Too bad Wilson passed away some years back. He was a good man." Jackson added, "And, yes, Uncle Phillip could really tease."

You Need to Get Out of Here

Will laughed, and then apologized, saying, "You were talking about when you came back from the service . . ."

Jackson said, "Yeah. I ran around for some months after I got out, then holed up at Mom and Dad's place for a few weeks. I had been there maybe a week when Uncle Phillip came over. We sat outside and visited, he asked me how I was doing, if I was okay. He didn't press me, but we talked a bit about what we had each seen. We talked about all kinds of stuff, laughing about things like Wilson." Finally, Phillip got serious. "You know I wanted to pass on these medicines, these songs. I had thought maybe that might be you."

Jackson told him he remembered, and Phillip continued, "*Huhn.* I have been thinking about it. A lot. One day, while you were gone, I had a dream, I call it a dream, but it was real. I was awake, but in that other place, where medicines live. I was looking to find out what was happening to us. I was talking to one of our medicines, but the medicine was in Spirit form. We were looking for something, something that was causing troubles on our side. We came to a place when we saw it, a house, a dwelling, but it had a darkness about it. The Spirit told me to wait. Then the Spirit, the medicine, went to the house, slowing as it approached the front. It stopped at the door, then went inside. A moment later, the Spirit came out, moving fast toward me, running, looking worried. It got to me and shouted, 'You need to get the hell out of here!'" Uncle said, "With that, I was back in this world."

Jackson continued, "Phillip laughed and said, 'I never heard a Spirit swear before that.' Phillip sat there for a while, smoking his cigarette, thinking about the dream, I guess. Then Uncle Phillip got serious, 'The more I thought about it, the more I understood. You're a good man, Jackson, our people are going to need you in the future. We've taught you things we will need. How to light the fire, how to wash at funerals. Give tobacco. But what I wanted to teach, it's hard. It demands a lot. Once you know these things, you can't go back, you can't refuse any of our people. If they ask for help, you must give it. No matter who it is, even if you don't like them. There are also things, like the house I saw, that you must prepare for, for what might be inside. I think that it is time to put my things, the things that I have, away. Our people aren't even learning our language. I haven't heard any kids speaking Euchee in twenty-five years. This is nothing to play with. You should focus on what we still have: our dances, our funerals, some of the other things. I wish you had come along twenty-five years ago. But, if you go over there, to where I was, then those things can come over here. Like at our funeral feast, if you're not strong enough to doctor the door and close it, then . . . maybe it is time for us to move on with our ways."

Some months after that, Uncle passed away.

Will and I sat there after Jackson was done. I asked Jackson what he thought about it. Jackson said, "Well, at the time I was disappointed. But the older I get, the more I understand. Uncle Phillip was right, ours was a hard way, it still is. Uncle may have told nasty, crazy stories, but Uncle Phillip really, deeply, believed in his ways, our ways. He was right, it's not anything to play with. Maybe we did need to get the hell out of that house," Jackson laughed. "He put those things away because he believed in them. So, that was all I learned about doctoring."

With that, Jackson was done with his story. I suspected, though, it wasn't the only thing he learned about doctoring, but I didn't ask him any more about it. A few minutes later, the women returned with coffee, and we sat waiting for the dance to start.

Shaggy—Indians Don't Get Lost

It was hot. Oklahoma in August hot. Still. Humid. Sunny. Hot. I had been in Phoenix during the summer for a meeting. Why the BIA would ever schedule a meeting in Phoenix in July was beyond me. Probably someone had a cousin who managed the casino. That was hot. I know, everyone says, "But it's a dry heat." Hell, 112 degrees is hot, dry or not. Be worse if it had been humid, but still hot. I would probably take that over today. Ninety-eight, maybe a hundred degrees. And humid. Thankfully, though, not humid like Florida. Or Wisconsin.

Damn, Wisconsin in summer in the woods could be brutal, too. Running around the rez, in the woods. Maybe not much over 80 degrees, but the humidity is so high, no wind, air so heavy and still in the forest. Beautiful with all that green and the cool, clear streams. But you get into the woods and encounter the humidity and stifling stillness. The sweat pouring off me, jeans soaked in no time, sweat stinging my eyes. And the damn mosquitoes, they could drive a fisherman off the river. We bitch about mosquitoes in Oklahoma, but we have no idea how bad they can be. Little tiny assassins eating your sanity. They build and build all the while you try to ignore them. "Don't think about them. Don't think about them." Saying that over and over till you can't think about anything else. Finally, you just give up and flee the woods as you hear them buzzing "Victory!" The woods belong to them, not us.

It's worse if you're lost. Like that time with Shaggy. Everyone called him Shaggy, or Shag, which had nothing to do with his looks. It was a shortened mispronunciation of his Indian name. Most probably didn't know his white man name, or his proper Indian name, but Shaggy fit him. He lived a bit away from the small rez town, not as remote as some places, but still pretty quiet. I must have been about twenty-three, running around the rez that summer in between school and staying at friends' places. Well, okay, more staying at friends' moms' and aunts' places, but they always liked me for some reason. Anyway, Shaggy wanted to look for some kind of medicine that day—can't remember what, but he said it was flowering now. So off we went across the road from where his aunt lived and into the woods. Shaggy said everything in his life happened in the woods. He was about ten or fifteen years older than me and grew up on the rez, but he had spent a lot of time with his mom's people in Minnesota. All the time he spent with his old uncles and aunts meant he knew a lot of old stories, some medicines, and spoke pretty good Indian, spoke really well after a few beers, which meant he spoke really well most of the time . . . for a young person. Young meant anyone under seventy. A guy could be sixty-five years old and still be called Sonny. True for Shaggy's rez, true for us in Oklahoma.

He had talked me into going with him that day. I had nothing else to do anyway, so off we went. We walked through the woods for the better part of an hour. He claimed we were following an old trail, but I never saw any path, but who knows? I didn't get out into the woods that often. Still, you get a feeling when you're lost even if you are a "city Indian," as he called me. Like how it seemed we had crossed that same little stream four times. Or that a clearing looked an awful lot like the one we saw about thirty minutes ago, or the one we went through an hour ago. This was long before cell phones, so there was no GPS to check, and no respectable Indian carried a compass because, as Shag said, "We don't get lost!" Yeah, sure, never get lost. I might not get into the woods much, but I knew there weren't that many little streams by his aunt's place.

Finally, the mosquitoes had driven my patience away.

"We're lost, aren't we?" I said to Shaggy when we came to an opening.

"Naw."

"That's the fourth damn time we crossed that stream," I told him.

"Naw, we good," Shaggy repeated as he kept walking.

I followed Shag. Not like I had a choice. I didn't know the way back, so off we went. The mosquitoes weren't getting any better, and we were both soaked in sweat. Besides, I guess Shag hadn't found his medicine.

About thirty minutes later, we came to "another" little field and Shaggy stopped for a smoke.

"This is the same meadow we saw an hour ago," I told him. "You're lost, aren't you." It wasn't a question.

Shaggy didn't even look at me, just lit his cigarette and said, "All these clearings look alike."

I thought, "What the hell??" The mosquitoes were getting to me, and I was getting tired.

As he puffed his smoke, we heard a voice, "You boys having fun?" We looked over, and sitting on a log along the tree line was Shaggy's uncle. His uncle said, "I was just thinking you guys should be coming through here again." We walked over to him, and he said, "I was kinda having fun watching. This is the third time I saw you guys go by."

"I was trying to teach him that trail," Shag said, glancing at me, telling his uncle, "But you know he spent too much time in school, he just don't learn."

I shook my head and said, "Damn it, Shag."

"Hmm. I would have guessed you were both lost," his uncle said, looking at me and back at Shaggy. He stubbed out his cigarette and said, "I'm going to head back. Your aunt probably has fixed something to eat. Would you mind walking me back?" He paused before adding with a grin, "You know, just to be sure an old man doesn't fall. Or get lost . . ."

"Yes, I guess we could do that. I can show him the trail another time," Shag answered.

As we started off, I thought that for an old man, Shaggy's uncle moved through the woods *fast*, especially since he didn't seem to be hurrying. I was walking just behind him, and after a bit, he turned to me with a grin and said, "Amazing how these meadows all look alike, don't they?" That was the only thing he said on our way back. It took about fifteen minutes for his uncle to lead us to the road.

That was a hot and still day in the woods. A few years later, I heard that while Shaggy was visiting his relations up in the Twin Cities, he had been shot and killed. I never heard the details. It was just another Indian killed in the Cities. No big news, no big investigations. I still think about Shaggy sometimes. That day, though, was a good day.

Billy and the Indoor Dance

I have been told our Old People used to say you shouldn't take our dances out there, in the public. "If you want to dance, you have a place to dance," they used to say. By that, they meant if you want to stomp dance, just dance at our grounds. Anyway, that's what I've heard they used to say. But now a lot of people like these indoor stomp dances. Some of those Creek chiefs down south are still pretty set against indoor dances, though you see some other chiefs hosting or attending them. Best I can tell, most other tribes didn't have the same restrictions we used to about these dances. Maybe it never was the same for them, maybe stomp dance was always more social to those other Indians. This, though, is our religion. I'm not sure when this started to change for our people, but nowadays some of our people really like indoor dances. Even if we do indoor dances, we are still supposed to respect it. We're supposed to take it seriously. I admit they are fun; the fellowship and the singing are something we all miss during the winter months. Maybe it is just a chance to socialize. Whatever the reason, indoor stomp dance has its following.

Billy was one of those. He was good about attending the dances. And he did his share of work at the grounds, for the most part. He liked to lead and was a good one. But he liked those indoor dances. I think part of the reason he liked them was because he often was asked to organize or host these indoor dances, to put on exhibition dances as we call them. For those, he always got paid and would bring along a few helpers. He never did say exactly how much he got for those exhibitions. I noticed, however, that Billy's helpers never seemed to get as much as he did. Sometimes the only ones at those small exhibitions were white people. Often the white churches were the ones who wanted some Indians to put on an exhibition stomp. Sometimes those white people would then later ask if we knew Billy. They would tell us how they had met him, and he was so "spiritual." They just loved him. I was with Jackson the first time that happened, and Jackson just stood there and said, "Hmmm . . ." That was it. I knew Jackson didn't like it, but he would never say anything.

We'd heard about one such dance from Jackson's niece. She was a good kid in her early twenties and had a little girl. Jackson had tried to gently tell her maybe she shouldn't do those dances, but he never pushed too hard on what one should or shouldn't do. He wouldn't go to them, but he wouldn't really criticize others for attending. Unless they ever tried to do our main day medicine dances, then I don't think he would have been quiet. Anyway, maybe she listened to Jackson, but who knows? This particular time, she probably went with Billy because she needed money for her little girl. You could tell she didn't want to tell Uncle Jackson because she was embarrassed about it. Billy wanted to put on some social dances, and those used gourd rattles. Actually, now we make our gourds out of coconuts, but we still call them gourds. They probably were gourds in the old days, but no one around us grew those gourds, probably hadn't grown them in a long time.

Billy managed to round up five or six men and women for this dance, mostly young people in their teens and early twenties. They all showed up that day and were ready to slip on their Indian clothes—ribbon shirts and vests for the men, and ribbon dresses for the women. Of course, if it had been a real stomp dance, not many of the men would have been wearing anything besides jeans, T-shirts, or maybe regular shirts and just ribbon skirts for the women. But that didn't look very Indian, so they always dressed up for these exhibitions. Thus, there they were, waiting around for Billy to do his little talk and start the dance. Jackson's niece said, finally, Billy starts talking to the people, some white church in Tulsa. It seemed like those white churches always loved Indian dances. I'm not sure why. Maybe it was their white guilt? It seemed they couldn't get enough of Indian things to look at. These churches were always either trying to cast out our demons for being pagans or wishing they were us, sometimes both. Not that most of them would ever do anything to help our ability to continue their ways. A few of the churches were socially active, but mostly they just felt better about themselves after they saw the Indians dance. But at least they cared.

Anyway, Jackson's niece told us Billy finally got done explaining about the social dance, and she is waiting to dance, they are all waiting to start dancing. They're lined up, ready, looking at Billy, wondering when he will start, wondering when he will raise the gourd to begin. They don't see any gourd. The white people don't know what's going on, but those Indians did. They're looking at him and whispering to each other, "Where's the gourd?" Billy looks panicked. Another minute passes as Billy runs to his backpack and digs around. Finally, Billy digs in his pocket and pulls out his phone. Jackson's niece said she and the other dancers were wondering who is he going to call? No way anyone can get here that fast with a gourd. Then Billy comes back to them and straightens up and lifts his phone in the air. He has a recording of gourds on his phone. Jackson's niece and the others look at one another again, embarrassed now and at the same time nervously trying not to laugh. The white people don't know anything is wrong, but the stomp dancers sure do. They are all thinking, "What the . . . ?"

Billy starts singing and dancing to his cell phone gourd. The Indians look at one another, give a shrug, and start following him. They all do that for the next two dances, and the white people start joining in. There they were in the church hall, Billy, his phone, the stomp dancers, and the white people going around a flashlight on the floor. Afterward, the church people were talking about how spiritual they felt dancing, how they were thankful the Indians had come to share their culture with them. Meanwhile, Niece and her friends were thinking they just wanted to get their money from Billy and get the heck out of there. But they stuck around visiting, trying to act nice with those white people.

Jackson shook his head listening to the story, while Jackson's niece looked sheepish. She said, "I'm so sorry. You were right, Uncle. That is the last time I do an exhibition. I'm not much for cell phone dances."

Jackson nodded, told her he loved her and she had better go pick up her kid from school. After she left, Jackson leaned in toward me and said, "I'm not much of one for indoor dances, but it would have been kind of fun to see that phone dance. I might have learned something." I knew Jackson wouldn't say anything to Billy, but I knew for a fact I would mention it around Billy. This would follow him for a very long time. From then on, whenever he pulled out his phone at the grounds, someone would always laugh and ask what model gourd he had.

Billy Plans to Doctor Dzehne

Everybody said Dzehne was a good dog, and why wouldn't they? He thought of himself as a pretty good dog, maybe not great, but certainly good. Dzehne was a typical Indian dog, mid-sized, nondescript black-and-white mottling. Dzehne always let Jackson know when someone was at the door and let people know this was not a house to be messed with. But he had never bitten anybody. Yet.

Today he was listening to his master, Jackson. Well, he didn't really think of Jackson as his master, more as a good companion or friend who fed and took care of him. He couldn't remember a time without Jackson. He was just a pup when they started living together. Jackson's wife, Mary, always said Jackson spoiled him. Dzehne noticed, however, that it was Mary who saved the scraps from the table and snuck them to him when she thought Jackson wasn't paying attention. All and all, it was a pretty good life for a dog.

Dzehne didn't worry about much, but he was beginning to wonder if he should. Tonight, Dzehne was lying there, looking half asleep, but he always knew what was going on in and around the house. Jackson's friend Bear had come over to visit. Bear was a big man, tall, bulky, with long hair. Bear knew a lot of stories and was usually willing to tell funny ones about himself. He had been in more than a few scraps when he was young, which meant he was also missing a few teeth, but this didn't stop him from having a grin most of the time. But as most who knew Bear said, he looked better than those who had messed with him ended up looking. Dzehne always liked Bear, maybe it was his smell, or that he liked to talk to Dzehne, or that Bear scratched him behind his ears. Maybe it was because Dzehne thought he and Bear were alike, fun to be around but just a little bit dangerous.

Today, though, Jackson and Bear were talking about another one of their friends, Billy. Dzehne didn't particularly like that friend. He didn't trust him. He remembered one time when Billy thought Jackson wasn't looking, and Billy tried to kick Dzehne. Dzehne still didn't know why Billy did that to him, he had just been lying there. Dzehne was a laid-back dog, but he defended himself, and he turned to bite Billy. No one was going to kick him and get away with it. After all, he was a good dog but, like Dzehne said, dangerous. That day he almost got his teeth into Billy, too, but Jackson jerked Dzehne back just before he got hold of Billy. Honestly, Dzehne had no idea Jackson was that quick! Billy just laughed, but Dzehne could tell Jackson wasn't happy, mostly with Billy, even though he told Dzehne, *"Nehjubada!* (Behave). Afterward, Jackson didn't seem upset about the incident. From then on, Dzehne kept extra alert around Billy. He figured if he would kick a dog, who knew what other kind of evil he might try to do. Sometimes when Billy visited, Dzehne would growl softly, making Billy look a bit nervous. Jackson would look at Dzehne but wouldn't say anything.

As Dzehne listened to the two men tonight, he figured they must not care that much for Billy either. As the two talked, Bear mentioned how Billy had tried to convince Chief that Billy should be appointed to lead next year's dances. Bear was upset about that. He didn't think Billy was the man for the job. Dzehne was in total agreement. Jackson told Bear not to worry about it. Even if Billy's family was campaigning for him to lead the dances, Billy would have to sober up enough to be there for the early dances, Jackson laughed, and that would never happen.

Bear just grunted and went on that Billy's sister said he was visiting an Indian doctor down south who was teaching Billy—Bear wasn't sure what—songs, medicines, or something. Anyway, that's what Bear heard and that's why he came to visit his friend.

Jackson said not to worry, it wasn't a problem. Bear looked concerned and said, "Well, if he learns to doctor, it could be trouble . . ."

Jackson reminded him that even though Bear had a thing for Billy's sister, she was crazier than Billy. And besides, Billy could barely understand a few words in Indian, let alone speak fluently. But Bear wasn't convinced.

Finally, Jackson said, laughing, "Aw hell, Billy couldn't doctor a dog in his backyard! You know that."

"Yeah, I guess," Bear said after thinking about it, and started laughing, too.

Now Dzehne got worried listening to them talking about Billy. Dzehne didn't feel sick, why would someone be trying to doctor a dog, he thought? Or was he trying to hurt some other dog? Jackson and others would tell some of those old stories, about people changing into owls and other things. That got him worried. What if he got doctored and turned into a squirrel? Or maybe a cat? At that he snarled a little.

Jackson heard Dzehne. "You okay, boy?" and looked at Dzehne, "You hear something?"

"*Huhn, ahe dilahnhuhn,*"[2] Dzehne thought. But he just wagged his tail and looked at Jackson to let him know he had it under control. Thinking about it, Dzehne really wished he had gotten his teeth into Billy that day. He decided right then that if he got the chance to bite Billy, he would. Dzehne started thinking about it and could almost smell Billy's fear, which made Dzehne wag his tail more. That would teach Billy to doctor dogs, in the backyard or anywhere else. As he started enjoying that thought, Bear got up to leave.

"Well, next time," Jackson said to Bear.

"*Huhn,*" Bear answered and left.

Jackson asked Dzehne how he was doing and if he wanted a treat, which of course he did. All was good again. Still, Dzehne decided next time he'd get one good bite in Billy because even a dog doesn't like to get doctored without permission.

Soup Dance and Chief

As I said earlier, Polecat Euchee Ceremonial Grounds is the main stomp ground of the three Euchee grounds. It is the fireplace we brought with us from Georgia to Indian Territory in the 1830s. The coals, the embers, the medicines are the same ones we've had since the very beginning. For us ceremonial people, Green Corn is the focal point of ceremonial life, our new year, and the highlight of our Euchee year. The week leading up to July's Green Corn is always busy. Families, or groups of families, will each have a camp. Before we were removed from Georgia in the 1830s, Euchee lived in an actual tribal town setting, our family homes were probably our camps. Now these are our homes during the ceremonial dances. Currently we have some twenty-plus camps at Polecat, open air, set around the stomp grounds. Families must clean their camps and also help some of the elderly fix their camps. The camps used to be brush arbors, but now many use tarps to cover their eating area. Some have put up slightly more permanent tops. But a few of us still cling to using willow brush–topped arbors. There is a reason for that, but we understand that as one gets older, compromises must be made to get through Green Corn. Putting up your camp with brush is a lot of work, and if you don't have healthy menfolk to help, it won't get done. Besides the arbors, each camp has a place for cooking, usually an open fire enclosed by bricks and a grate top, along with maybe propane camp stoves. Then tables and storage shelves for pots and pans, canned goods, cooking utensils, and everything else you need to run an outdoor event kitchen. Then, of course,

Dinner table, Bigler camp, Polecat Euchee Stomp Ground, July 2018.

there are parking spots, places to sit, and tables. All a great mix of things brought to our grounds every year just to get through the sixteen days of Green Corn.

It is a task just trying to remember everything we need to do for Green Corn, the main medicine day: rebuild our hill at sunup on Friday morning, take care of grounds business all day Friday, and dance a half night that evening. If you are lucky, you get maybe a couple hours' sleep Friday night. Green Corn Day itself makes for a very long day. We set up in the arbors at the square grounds before sunup Saturday, watch the pole boys clean last year's ashes and start the fire, dance all day while fasting. Ribbon Dance late that afternoon, then Buffalo Dance. Finally getting to eat, break our fast, after dusk. Then stomp dance all Saturday night, not finishing till after sunup Sunday. Those Old People, the ones who have gone on, used to say you need to stay up till sundown Sunday night after Green Corn to make the medicine strong. I am lucky if I make it to noon Sunday before passing out from exhaustion. Happy and fulfilled, but exhausted.

As I got older, I realized that for us who are there all year, the hard work of getting to this main day was done. Work parties, ball games, sharpening chainsaws, looking for medicines, checking with the Creek Nation for trash containers and sanitation and funds, talking to campers, getting those early dances done when we didn't have much help. That's what filled the months leading up to Medicine Day. At Green Corn, we had so many visitors at our camps, all our families and friends coming to look on and help, so many people for whom this was likely the only time they could attend during the year. Campers are excited to see everyone return home to Polecat, but Green Corn is still exhausting.

The week after Green Corn, we stay camped-in all week, keeping our medicine fire, Grandfather, burning day and night. The pole boys feed it so it never goes out between when we rebuild it at sunup Green Corn Saturday morning till Sunday morning eight days later. That week might not be hard work, but it takes commitment. Not only from our pole boys but from our campers and our ceremonial grounds to support everything that needs doing. It affirms the importance of what we do. That we are still here, that we continue. A covenant with the Creator. No one will do it for us. The week after Green Corn we are supposed to be at our camps, representing the family or extended family. That week in the evenings, the camps are supposed to be "lit," having someone there. Probably only about half the members will camp in throughout the week because of work or because the campers live far away from the grounds. But the others continue by feeding the pole boys, cooking supper, or just being at the grounds to visit one another.

A few years back, when our previous chief was still with us, maybe on Wednesday or Thursday of that Soup Dance (or Campers) week, Chief and I were sitting in the west arbor, the Chiefs' arbor, on the square grounds. Our menfolk had rebuilt the ground's arbors two weeks earlier for Arbor Dance, using post oak or hickory for the support forks and cross poles and covered with willow for shade. That particular evening, it was just the two of us sitting there, just about dusk. We were watching Grandpa fire, at the center of the grounds, burning as it does that entire Green Corn week. The campers were starting to fix supper. Most of them won't eat till the sun goes down, waiting for that little bit less hot to arrive. Nothing too big or fancy for dinner. That big meal had been Green Corn a few days before. But we might welcome a few visitors to our tables, usually just other campers stopping by to visit. During Medicine Day, we are all too busy to get around to the other camps: the menfolk on the square ground; the women preparing for the evening meal, watching the children, and preparing for Ribbon Dance, taking care of the camps. The week after, though, is just the home bunch, the ones who get us through all those ball games, work parties, and first few dances.

By dusk, our camps were lit with the yellow glow of lanterns, as we haven't allowed electricity at our grounds. Chief and I could hear the members moving about, their occasional laughter wafting from the camps up to the square grounds, to the Chiefs' arbor. The children were running and playing. We could see the teens walking around and around the outside of the grounds on the dirt and gravel road, as they had for as long as we could remember. Chief and I just sat there, listening and watching the camps and our members, watching Grandpa fire.

Chief and I sat there enjoying the evening. We could feel this Euchee life, our families and children, our homes, our fireplace. It is hard to explain or understand, but I was proud to know we still had a chief for our Euchee life. Someone who was there to lead us, traditionally lead. At dusk, when people and shadows merge at the center of our ceremonial world, the physical and spiritual are quietly joined, we could hear the life in our camps. When we looked toward the camps surrounding the grounds, we could see our people, both past and future. Maybe things were different from what used to be, but we were still doing what we were supposed to, just as we were fifty or a hundred years before.

I wondered how many tribal people had this stolen from them over the years. We were blessed to still hold on to our Green Corn, to our ceremonies. We are a small, little-known tribe. Even most other Indians have no idea about us or our dances. I turned to Chief and said, "Unless someone sees this, they have no idea what we do. You should be proud. Your people are still here."

Chief didn't say anything, he just looked around and nodded as we sat there, listening and watching. It was dusk and wouldn't be long till evening arrived. The children and teens would soon come up to the square grounds to have their night of practice dancing. In a few days, in a week, we might go back to life outside the square grounds. But at that moment, in this place, we were doing what we were supposed. It was good to be Euchee.

Chief Comingdeer's Nephew

I usually don't write about particulars involving our ceremonial grounds, as some things are better discussed in person or learned by doing. However, some are interested in our ceremonial way of life, and perhaps others may find encouragement in hearing about our ways. So, while I won't go into details, and with the permission of my friend, I will share a story from a few years ago.

Over the last thirty-five years, I often was the *goshti-shone*, stickman, at Polecat, usually carrying stick to start the night. The *goshti-shone* is the one who runs the stomp dance, picking leaders, making sure things are done right. At the start of the night, Chief picks one of the men to carry stick. Sometimes, if it's a big dance, two men will be appointed to take care of the crowd, especially during Green Corn. For us, the sticks are rivercane, about four feet long; I'm not sure what other grounds use. That stick represents, I was told, the chief's authority. When you carry stick, you carry out Chief's directions, you are running the dance for him. Not that he tells the *goshti-shone* what to do, though he sometimes does, but that is what that stick represents.

Carrying stick has rules one must follow and enforce, small rules and some big ones. Those rules may differ between grounds, but they are similar overall. However, some grounds may be stricter about enforcing their rules. We try to follow and enforce the rules as we know them.

As I ask our younger ones, do you feel more pride knowing others say Polecat is kind of strict or hearing people say you can just do whatever you want up there?

Carrying stick is not, generally, a hard job as jobs at our grounds go. But sometimes people get mad because you tell them they are not allowed to do something. They can't dance like that, or having to pull the occasional drunk out of the dance because we do not allow such behavior. And, of course, the night gets long: being on one's feet the whole time, checking on the crowd, sometimes dancing on the outside of the ring, going out around the edges of the grounds in the dark to find the next leader, and so forth. Usually, I carried stick when we started our dances, which could be any time from about 10:00 P.M. to sometimes starting closer to midnight. About halfway through the dance, around 3:00 or 4:00 A.M., Chief would have me turn the stick over to someone else to carry it till morning. I'm getting older, so maybe I will be retired from that job. I have other things I do to help, so that is okay. But it is always an honor to be *goshti-shone*. Whatever I can do to help get us through.

As often happens during our first dance, one year we had a small home crowd—mostly just our ground members with a few visitors. Sonny Brown was our chief at Polecat back then. I really liked Sonny, he was a quiet man, a few years older than me, a Vietnam veteran whose dad had been chief before him. As usual, Sonny had me start out carrying stick. Around 4:00 A.M., I was getting tired and went over to the Chiefs' arbor. I thought I would turn the stick in to Chief for him to give it to someone else to carry till we finished at sunup around 6:30 A.M. Then I would get a chance to sit down, rest for a bit, and enjoy the dance. After first getting some coffee of course.

I went up to Sonny where he sat in his chief's spot, in that west arbor, on that cold, hard, wooden log bench. I stood just to the side of him so he could still see the fireplace and dancers. I asked, "Chief, you want to let someone else have some of the fun and carry stick the rest of the night?"

Chief looked up, smiled, and told me, "Aww, you about got it. You good."

I stood there for a moment, shook my head, and simply said, "Okay."

There wasn't much else I could say. If Chief tells you you're good, then you're good. So off I went to pick the next stomp dance leader. I carried stick the rest of that night till the sun came up and we closed the door to quit dancing. Sonny always thought that was pretty funny.

A couple years after that, we again had a small crowd at one of the early dances. We were blessed, though, with a few visitors from several other grounds, including one of the Cherokee grounds. David Coming-deer was their chief and a friend of ours. That night he brought with him several of his Cherokee leaders and shell shakers. Luckily for me, this night around 3:30 A.M. Chief let me turn the stick and duties over to another of our men. I handed the stick back to Chief, who gave it to the new *goshti-shone*. I shook Chief's and the next *goshti-shone*'s hands. Then I went to Chief's camp to take a little break before finding a seat under the arbor to enjoy the dance.

Chief's sisters ran the camp and always kept hot coffee and food to feed the visitors and for anyone else that got hungry during the night. I always enjoyed that short break after carrying stick but didn't like to take too long or else I would get lazy and sleepy. David, the Cherokees' chief was there, getting some coffee. He always tried to make our dances, and we got to his dances over by Tahlequah whenever we could. David had a couple of his members with him, including his young nephew Adaya (Cherokee for "Red Oak"), who was maybe seven or eight years old at the time. His nephew was eating, maybe soup or maybe a dessert. David introduced his nephew, and I asked Adaya if he led. He shook his head no.

I teased him, "Now that you ate at our chief's camp, you have to lead. That's how you pay for your meal. That's how we Euchee do things."

He looked at me and then at his uncle David, who told him, "That's how it is. Now you have to lead."

"Really?" he asked.

David and I both laughed and said, "Oh yes, that's how it is."

Adaya smiled and said he had never led before but could try.

I laughed again and told him, "I'll tell the new stickman."

David and I visited awhile longer, finished our break, and returned to our spots. I found my replacement and told him that David's young nephew was sitting over there with the Cherokees, and he would go if asked. Sure enough, after a while I saw the little boy coming out to the fire to lead, his uncle and the other Cherokee leaders and shell shakers following behind. We Polecats all got up and went out to help him, too. You could tell he was a little unsure, but he did well. He got through his songs just fine.

After he was done and sitting down again, I went over to thank him and shake his hand. I told him he did great leading. I visited with David for a bit about when they would dance next, when we would probably hold Green Corn. Before I went back to my arbor to sit down, I told the boy, "From now on, if anyone asks you if you lead stomp dance, you tell them yes."

Those Cherokees came back to our dance the next Friday night, and we had another small home crowd. I made certain to pick David's nephew to lead, and again he did well. Afterward, his uncle told me that on the way home from our dance that first night, Adaya said he could do that "a thousand more times."

I hope Adaya comes back to our grounds for many years. I hope Polecat will still be dancing in the future. That we will still be there to help him get some of those one thousand times when he leads. I hope that Adaya will visit Polecat as an old man, when he is in his seventies or eighties. Then, whoever is our chief in that future will, as our chiefs sometimes do in the morning after we have finished our dance and the sun is rising, our chief might ask if any of the visitors would like to speak. To say something to the people. Perhaps that boy, now an old man, will stand up and tell the story of how when he was young, he came to Polecat with his uncle David and got to lead for the very first time.

The way things are at our grounds today with people working, living away, and sometimes just falling away from participation, we sometimes have a small home crowd at the early dances. We are always thankful to have visitors but especially at the early dances. Sometimes, when only one or two visitors come, they may think they are not helping much. But to us, even one or two additional leaders or shell shakers helps us, making a long night easier. They lift our spirits, and we always appreciate them.

We are blessed with fine young boys and girls at the ceremonial grounds, at Polecat and at our friends' grounds. We thank the Creator for our young ones, the few elders we still have, and the visitors with whom we get to share our dances. My old chiefs used to say, "It's hard being Indian." But they also said, "It's good to be Euchee."

Wado to Chief Comingdeer for allowing us to borrow his nephew. That night was a promise between us to help one another. Perhaps both of our peoples can keep our ways alive for a while longer. This is what our ceremonial way of life means.

After the Dance—Whose Kid Is This?

Like so many stomp-dance families during the summer, back twenty, thirty years ago, when we got home from a dance, we never knew whose kids we would end up with at the house, or now whose grandkids. My wife is from a northern tribe, pow-wow people. When we first got married, we used to go to pow-wows up north and sometimes down here. She moved to Euchee Country when we married, and from then on, it was mostly stomp for us. We would still occasionally go to a pow-wow. We would laugh that we were going "to watch the Indians." Funny, because we were ceremonial people, yet we, too, fell into the narrative that somehow "real Indians" pow-wowed, stomp-dance life not being part of what people thought of when imagining Indians. We have a lot of friends and some relations who are pow-wow people, and we have fun when we go. It just wasn't our thing, or at least my thing, and she supported my commitment.

Stomp dance for our people is not social, though that is part of it. It is religious, sacred, social, cultural; we jokingly say stomp dance is life, but it is in fact just that, life. Stomp dance is tied to the Green Corn ceremonies we were given by Gohahtine, the Giver of Breath, the Creator. It takes dedication for those of us who keep our grounds alive, and we have deep connections to the other ceremonial people who manage to keep their tribal fireplaces going. We still take our medicines despite all the forces mustered against us. We have seen and know the other grounds that once were and are no more. Our old tribal towns with our chiefs, camps, and ceremonies form our religion, our blood, an entire way of

116

life. When we talk among ourselves, we always marvel at how outsiders have no idea what we do, that this still goes on. Even other Indians to the west of us, full-blood tribal members, don't know this stomp-dance world exists. Maybe they've observed a few social stomp-dance exhibitions put on at a pow-wow, probably indoors. That is not us.

In the spring, our grounds will start by holding four Indian football games over four or five Sundays. We then dance six weekends, with Green Corn being three weeks in a row, with us camped-in during that time. On the weekends that we don't dance, we might go to one of the other ceremonial grounds to visit and help them, supporting one another. Might be another Euchee grounds, or maybe a Muscogee, Cherokee, or Shawnee grounds.

On stomp-dance weekends, my wife and I would load up our daughters, and now our grandkids, and head to our grounds for the dance. We would get there before suppertime when it was still light. Chief usually had things for me to do, so I tried to get there early. I would do whatever he needed or maybe we would just sit under the arbor, visiting, making the calls after dark to tell the members to gather at the grounds so we could start, then dancing till sunup. In the morning, after our regular dances (not during Green Corn), we would load up our stuff, folding chairs and such, in the back of the truck, find the girls, and with luck head for home by 7:00 A.M. or so to get some sleep. I would get to bed maybe around 8:00 A.M. However, I always seemed to wake up by 11:00 A.M. or noon. I wanted to sleep later but never did.

When I got up, I would start some coffee and then check on our girls. I would, hopefully, find our two lying there. It was always a mystery as to which other stray girls I might find in our kids' room. We usually seemed to end up with a few extra from the grounds. Or sometimes we were short one of our girls. I would forget that my wife or I had given in at some point during the night when someone had begged to come home with us or stay at someone else's place. I would see two or three in the bed and sometimes one or two on a pallet made of blankets on the floor. Kids strewn everywhere. I'd check with my wife. I might kind of recognize the kids, but my wife would know their names and who the parents, aunts, or grandparents were that raised them. From there, I knew their family, their grandparents, great-grandparents, which grounds they belonged to or where their family had lived, and family history. My wife and I split the two-step process of keeping track of these stomp-dance kids. After the summer ended, it would be six or eight weeks before we sorted all the stray laundry and returned it to the proper owners. My wife would do wash and ask, "Whose shirt (or shorts, socks, etc.) are these?" We would get a muffled "dunno," but eventually we would return things and get our daughters' stuff back. Our grounds shared kids, clothes, and food even after we left summer behind. I was surprised we never ended up with an extra dog or two.

Two or three years back, my wife and I were at the grounds before supper, that time around dusk when there is still light out but the campers are getting the lanterns ready, and the whippoorwills are just starting to sing. There were a few home bunch and a couple of visitors from another grounds sitting around eating, or drinking coffee, and visiting. One of our daughter's friends, a young woman about thirty years old, was there. She grew up at the grounds but fell away from it in her twenties but had now started coming to the dances again. She was remembering when she was little and came to all the dances with her mom and dad. In the morning after we finished, she loved going home with us to hang out with all the girls at our place. She went on that we always had the best snacks, and we let them watch VCR movies all afternoon, laughing at that, saying, "Who even has a VCR now?"

After she left to go sit by her sister on the south edge of the grounds, I told my wife, "I don't remember her coming over to the house."

My wife reminded me that she and her sister, or one of the other stomp-grounds' girls, would beg to come over. They would all pile into the truck, and "when we got home, they'd all be asleep in the back seat, and you'd make two trips carrying them all in from the truck," my wife laughed.

I shrugged and said, "I guess. I didn't know which kids we had. We usually managed to bring ours home, though, right?"

My wife laughed, "Usually. Though sometimes Sis would bail out on us and we might still end up with a few little guests."

We still collect strays, though now we are on our second or maybe third generation, depending on how you measure. We went to a dance last summer and our granddaughter's friend Lil begged to come home with us. Lil was short for little KZ, her mom was big KZ, or really Cassie, but no one ever seemed to be called by their real names. Her mom, big KZ, is Creek, belonging to one of the grounds down south. KZ works hard to make ends meet, a good woman and younger than us. My wife and I just love Lil and her mom, they are always so entertaining. My wife was saying that KZ goes through boyfriends pretty quick. She's been married four times, though husband number one and three were the same guy, so we weren't sure if that counted as three or four times.

"We've been married thirty years, and you ran through three, maybe four, husbands in half that time," we would tease KZ. "What's with that?"

"I just want to get my money's worth," KZ responded.

My wife and I just shook our heads.

When we would see her and no one was by her side, we would ask, "What happened to your new man?"

She would look at us and respond, "He was stupid."

Which meant, of course, we had to ask, "Then why were you with him?" And we would all laugh. She never got upset at us for teasing her.

KZ was always happy to have her daughter stay with us, sometimes a night would stretch into a week till the next dance, where we would exchange kids. Besides keeping our granddaughter busy when we were tired, we figured if we brought her daughter home, we could catch up on big KZ's adventures.

We would ask, "So, Lil, what's the story on your mom's new man?"

She would say, "He's some guy in Tulsa."

"Is he Indian?"

"Yay, some western tribe. Something pow-wow."

"Dang, girl, you don't know?" my wife would ask.

"Umm, not sure. I think he's got a couple kids," Lil shrugged and added, "younger than me."

I looked at Lil and asked, "You don't know how many? How about their names?"

"I don't know. Why ask them? They'll be gone before I can remember their names, so why bother," Lil shrugged again, continuing to dig around in our fridge.

My wife and I laughed, "That's cold, girl!"

"Well, it's true. You know my mom." Lil stood up, turning to look at us, "The kids' names are something like Bobby, Billie, Mary, whatever. It don't matter. They're already history. They just don't know it yet. They're here, they're gone . . ."

With that, Lil and our granddaughter found something to eat, grabbed it, went back to their room and phones. Some things about stomp-dance life never seem to change.

Fixing Medicine for Funerals

At some point, Jackson realized he had become "one of the old guys" at the stomp grounds. He didn't think of himself that way. But he was getting to "that age." He didn't want to admit it, even though he got up with a groan in the morning and it took longer to get going for the day. Chief, well chiefs really, knew they could depend on Jackson to do what they asked of him, no worry about whether it would get done or done right. Chief asked his advice on things, too. He might not take the advice, but Chief would listen, and that was all Jackson expected. Jackson considered himself one of the worker bees and enjoyed that role. He would call Chief to visit, ask what was needed, or just how he was doing even when it was not dance season.

Chief was an old man, in his mideighties, yet he did more than most of the young men, first there and last to leave, always thinking about how this place could go on after he was gone. Jackson thought about that weight, about so many white people's romantic vision of Indian chiefs formed by novels, movies, or TV, of some romanticized caricature of Crazy Horse or Chief Joseph. Some young natives bought into that, too. Jackson knew, though, that we were blessed to still have the real thing. Chief spoke the language, knew the old ways and ceremonies; he was a quiet but tough man, determined but with a sense of humor that came out when you weren't expecting it. The more Jackson helped, the more Jackson was happy he didn't sit in Chief's seat. Young ones always wanted to be a chief, even some of the older ones. The more Jackson helped, the more he knew to leave that job to the real chief. Too

Cooking at Bigler camp, Polecat Euchee Stomp Ground, Green Corn 2021.

much responsibility for everything; Chief was always Chief: whenever, wherever, whomever, always Chief. Jackson shook his head when he thought about the weight Chief carried for everyone, keeping them moving forward at the grounds.

Despite Jackson's commitment to the grounds, most people depended more on his assistance for funerals. He often got called to fix the traditional medicine for people to wash with after the graveside service, him sitting with the can of medicine behind the church or home or wherever the service might be held. He knew how to do most of the things his people were supposed to do for funerals, at least those things we still did—the prayers, digging the grave, the talks, the little fire, placing restrictions on the family (when they wanted). He even knew, mostly, what the women were supposed to do. He had given the talk to the body a few times and would always do it if asked. But Jackson, selfishly he thought, preferred not to do that one. It was hard emotionally and spiritually. Talking to the body, preparing it for the work ahead. Telling it what it had to hear, what lay ahead—what was coming, what had to happen. When Jackson was young, Chief had told him what to say and do.

For Jackson, that was hard, but he did it. It was a thing one had to do by oneself for that person, and for the family. After Jackson made the talk for the first time, he thought of his uncle Phillip, about the old funerals and funeral feast his people used to hold, the last one back in the late 1960s. Uncle Phillip was a World War I veteran, an Indian doctor—a good one from what the Old People said. The training those Indian doctors received rivaled the white doctors' education, but we didn't have written textbooks. His uncle had been trained for years, starting as a boy till he was a young man and had to pass a "final test" in the woods. His uncle claimed he had to learn over four hundred songs and medicines from his grandpa and uncle. It was all done one-on-one, songs, stories, teachings, the plants, and their preparations. That kind of training just couldn't happen anymore, as young people weren't fluent in the old language and they didn't have the patience; it was a hard way to live, being an Indian doctor. Phillip always seemed to have a smile on him and knew about old things, really old things. Jackson wished he had spent more time with him, but Jackson knew he was lucky he learned what he did from his uncle.

Phillip had been in charge of funerals, and told him all the things that needed to be done, how the house was to be prepared, what had to be doctored, how the last feast was laid out, and how he closed up the home in the evening, doctoring the door while he pulled it closed, everyone staying up all night outside till the next morning when Phillip would go back in, prepare and open the house. At one time, his uncle had wanted to teach Jackson those doctoring songs for the funeral and feast, after Jackson got back from the service. But Jackson didn't learn them, maybe because he was too busy being young and a bit wild, or maybe because he wasn't supposed to learn them. For whatever reason, his uncle didn't teach him. Now Jackson thought sometimes that he should have, but he also knew he was not his uncle. Perhaps Uncle Phillip was right, it was time to put those other things away. If he was honest, the commitment those old Indian doctors had was more than he, or anyone, was capable of in this day and age. Jackson knew what he would've had to do, and not do. It could eat up a person if not obeyed. Those Old People were hard, not in the sense of mean, but strong, unrelenting. He was not sure, in Indian the word *dabale* translated as "hard" or "strong," so that is how he thought of those Old People. Doing the things that had to be done, they knew no other way. That is probably why some of our old things weren't lost, they just got put away. Those ways were nothing to be played with, and if not done right, there was a price to pay. Still, Jackson sometimes regretted not learning them.

To Jackson, it was not surprising that we had lost some traditional practices. Rather, it was amazing, a blessing, we still had so many. He felt proud of that, but he wondered for how much longer, as things seemed ready to slip away as fewer people paid attention, were too busy, moved away, or maybe just didn't learn. Some young men and woman paid attention, but it seemed like fewer and fewer as the years passed. Maybe things were starting to change, it seemed like some of these young ones were starting to pick up the language. He knew other tribes had lost more than we had, but he also knew some tribes held on to many of their ways. Jackson imagined every tribe did what they could, and all we could do was try to carry on what we knew. He wondered if someday someone would think about him the way he remembered Uncle Phillip.

One never knew when someone's time would come, so Jackson tried to always be ready for a funeral by having medicine on hand. He would go out in the late spring to gather it when it was easiest to find. He liked the early morning, just as the sun was coming up. He didn't know that he had to go out so early, but he preferred to do things when the day was new and the world waking up. He felt connected to the Old People and the old places when he went out. He thought it might be vanity to think that. Other times, he felt he was just doing the best he could with what he knew. The medicine was a fairly common plant and usually not hard to find. Sometimes, though, when Jackson started feeling self-important about his role, it hid on him. He would spend an entire morning looking only to find nothing, always a reminder to stay humble. He shook his head because he knew better than to be that way. The last time it happened, he mentioned it to Chief.

"I told you," the old man said, looking at Jackson with that smile of his.

"I know," Jackson responded, shaking his head.

"And you—almost an old man!" Chief teased.

"Yeah, I know. But I got a few years yet, so I'm good," as they both laughed.

Funerals were a time of loss and pain for the family. It was also one of the times the tribe came together. Green Corn was another such time, but not everyone participated in Green Corn, since many tribal members were Christian nowadays, and some simply didn't participate.

Funerals cut across all classes and groups. It seemed as though everyone wanted to be Indian when they passed away, wanting the medicine, the little prayers, the quilt—at least most wanted all these things.

Jackson would set up at dawn, getting things ready. He had a thirty-gallon galvanized can he used to fix the medicine in, which he kept put up with his other "Indian things," as his wife called them, in his shed. He had his favorite lawn chair he would bring and usually toss another one in the back of the truck in case a visitor came and forgot theirs. He would set up behind the church or home, to the west, if possible, out of the way. He tried to have the medicine sitting in the sun and might bring an easy-up tent for some shade if it was especially hot during the summer. During the winter, he might sit in his truck by the medicine, though sometimes he brought the easy-up during the winter, too, along with a propane heater to keep warm. It just depended. Other men would usually join him after a while, sitting there in their jeans, boots, and dress shirts. Sometimes he wore his cowboy hat, but a lot of times it would be an old ballcap.

He usually set up by himself. Sometimes they held the funeral at the small Indian church south of town, or maybe at the house if out in the country, where everyone headquartered. The family, friends, and relatives might stay up all night with the body after the wake service till the funeral the next day. That happened less and less now. If the funeral was held at the funeral home, the funeral home usually didn't let them stay in there all night. Anyway, it was kind of creepy to be in a funeral home in the middle of the night. It didn't bother Jackson to keep company all night in the country with relations that passed away, but being around dead white people? Those Spirits probably didn't know what was going on. *Gagas* (white people) were confused enough in life, but after death? No thank you, Jackson thought. When people did stay up, in the morning some of the men would come back and keep Jackson company after he got the medicine fixed. That's how he had learned, watching and sitting there, visiting with the old men. It was a chance to catch up with the others, telling stories, sometimes just sitting. Being with the medicine made them all think more about how things used to be, about people who had gone on, stories about the deceased (if they knew them), and what was going to happen. Of course, most of the time they just talked about everyday things like football or family, or about nothing at all.

If it was a wake and funeral for one of the more traditional families, there was always a lot of help. One or two of the women cooks would often bring a cot to sleep on so they could be up before sunrise to fix breakfast for the family and begin preparing the lunch or meal for attendees. A few would still stay up all night with the body, like they used to in the old days. For those who did, the women would leave out sandwiches, cookies, pie, or maybe some food, and always coffee, in case they wanted something in those dark middle-of-the-night hours. They'd get something to eat if they got hungry, food replacing sleep, like at dances. They would visit and talk, telling stories about the deceased and others, sometimes napping when no one was looking. A lot of history got told at three or four in the morning during those long nights. Nowadays, those who stayed up were usually few in number, and not all families did it even when they could.

There was always so much activity, but those who helped grew up with it in their lives and knew what needed doing. One time, Jackson remembered talking with his coworker, a *gaga-wenuh* (white man) a few years younger, about funerals and asking him how many he had attended. His friend said maybe 5 or 6—his parents, an uncle, a sibling, and a couple of friends. Jackson thought about it and figured he might have gone to 150–200 over the years. In a couple of bad years, he had been to 5 or 6 in a three-month period, when it seemed the Old People all died at the same time. So many connections, aunts, uncles, nieces, those who called him brother, friends, grounds members, all those Muscogee friends from the other grounds, and others—they all added up to a life of commitment to people you wanted to help in their times of need.

Jackson always learned something while sitting there. Maybe that was why, despite it being a funeral, he enjoyed those moments, feeling the old connections reaffirmed. Maybe they talked about who was related to whom, what happened in the past, or about why they did certain things. He wondered why more young guys didn't sit with them. Some of his nephews liked to talk about traditions and how the white man was stealing our culture, but Jackson thought more of them could actually sit and listen more. Oh well, Jackson thought, he was probably the same way when he was young.

He had learned a lot from those old men and old women, now gone. As he sat, he would think of those friends and relations, of them telling stories, smiling, and laughing. Sometimes serious, sometimes stories from way back, or maybe a crazy thing from their youth, but always continuing the bonds of community. Often friends from other tribes would come sit. Jackson liked that, he imagined it was the same way it had always been. We'd been friends with other tribes for a long time. It was good to know and share our pasts together and continue our history, which had so many similarities even in our differences. And there were, of course, a lot of intermarriages.

After the people got done with the funeral, finished at graveside, they'd all come back to wash off with the medicine. Sometimes that was before noon, like in the old days. Sometimes it was late afternoon, especially now when some preachers seemed to have a contest going on as to who could go the longest or wring the most emotions out of the family. Well, it was up to the family. So, what happened up front, as he would say, was up to them.

Jackson always waited till everyone finished washing off, till all the visitors were fed, and things started winding down before he would eat. He would drink coffee, sometimes water, throughout the day but wouldn't eat anything the day he washed people at a funeral. He thought maybe he shouldn't drink coffee either, but his uncle who had taught Jackson how to wash did, so Jackson drank it, too. Besides, coffee was almost like a medicine, maybe the best thing the *gaga* brought his people, Jackson laughed.

His wife often helped, along with a handful of the other women, with the cooking in the kitchen. They always checked on Jackson, seeing if he needed coffee or anything, letting him know everyone had eaten, telling him he had better eat now. Actually, sounding kind of bossy about him needing to eat, he thought. He would just nod and tell them he was okay, but he never left the medicine unattended.

His wife would just shake her head and tell her friends, "I told him to come eat, but he won't. That *gohane* is hardheaded, just plain stubborn." Her friends would laugh and say, "I mean!" but they all respected both of them.

Usually, one of the other men would sit there for a bit while he got something to eat or went inside for a minute. If no one was around, the women would bring him what he needed, coffee or food. He really didn't get that hungry sitting there, though the food always smelled good. It usually included what we considered our traditional foods: ham, pinto beans, pot roast, corn or green beans, hominy, corn soup, fried chicken, fried bologna, and lots of desserts. And if he was lucky, salt meat, and maybe his aunt would bring some of her cobblers, and baked beans with the bacon in it or her sour cornbread, though about half the time that was gone by the time he got to eat, unless one of the women "put a little aside" for him. Salt meat. He knew it was bad for him, but Jackson could not resist. He knew his joints would swell up from all the salt, he just hoped he didn't have a doctor's checkup the next day. It was something he didn't get every day, and his wife didn't make sour cornbread because it "smelled." Oh well, luckily his aunt would make them for funerals. His aunt was old, though, so he hoped some young women were learning how to make it. That would be tragedy to lose, he thought.

Jackson was always grateful for the women. He enjoyed hearing their laughter in the kitchen as they fixed lunch or the meal for after the graveside service. He was happy, proud really, that we still had women who knew how to take care of the women's side of things. He knew generally about those things, but left those to them, just as they left man business to him.

He remembered his aunt talking to his wife about when his aunt was young and they heard of a tribal member passing away. It didn't matter who it was that passed, if it was a tribal member, the Old People made the kids stay quiet, be respectful, no loud noises till after the funeral. She said several of the older women would gather at the deceased's house and clean it. His aunt also mentioned how they used to clean around the outside of the house, using four straw brooms. She explained an exact way that it was done and when, telling a story of how that came about and why. Jackson had never heard that before and asked when they stopped. She said maybe in the late 1940s or 1950s. She was sad to see that go. It seemed like such a good thing to do for the family, respectful, and not hard. After his aunt explained how they helped the family, several of the women asked his aunt if it would be okay to start again, and with her blessing and directions, they began reviving the practice. That made his aunt happy. It was a small thing, but one more way that was ours, Jackson thought. To Jackson, that is what made us a people. When these things slipped away, he thought, we simply became brown-white people, a reflection of what we had been but not the real thing. At least that is how Jackson felt.

Rain or shine, cold or heat, Jackson or one of the other men would take care of things. Most people didn't pay much attention to what or how—the medicine was always there. It seemed simple, a minor part of the funeral, and it was not difficult as long as one was willing to sit there for the day. Jackson, though, appreciated how it bound him and all the people to what they were given, the simple sacredness of it. How at least in one small part they continued to do something they had always done for as long as they had been who they were. He felt good to still have this, and though it only happened at moments when loved ones were lost, it helped the people and the tribe. It provided a measure of comfort and completion. For those who knew about it, though, it involved more—the old ways, tied to other things we did, sacredness, cleanliness, and Spirits. The small things sanctified their life. Such a simple act, so involved, Jackson thought, like so much else we did—simple looking but it could take half a day to explain and a lifetime of working to understand.

Dzoti Dodi

Euchee afternoons in April, we always meet in April.
    Year after year. Every year.
Time to head to the Grounds:
    the Hill, Kellyville, Polecat.
Cool Sunday afternoons, with white clouds and blue skies.
Sometimes dark clouds,
    rain wetting the ground.
Wondering if we will get rained out,
    but we never do.
That damp red clay, never coming out of your clothes.
Trying to get there early, Chief said 2:00 P.M.
We need hickory saplings for the ball goals.
    Not too thick,
    we have to bend them together to form an arch.
Chief says we used to tie them with the peeled bark.
Need to remember the twine,
    in the garage where I left it last year.
    Because we aren't going to strip those poles . . .
Driving out of Sapulpa,
    turning right on Highway 33,
    then left by the church.
Road 245, now paved, rougher now than when it was gravel.
    Turn in the gate, through the field a quarter mile.
    Tall weeds and grass creeping into the gravel drive,

129

hitting the side of the truck.
Slowly pull into our camp, avoiding the fallen limbs and brush.
Get out, grab my cap, and look around.
All the camps empty and overgrown.
The North Arbor—two cross poles fallen down,
    their dried willow brush no longer held up,
    splashing like a brown waterfall across the log benches below.
The Fireplace,
    last year's white ashes,
    now just a gentle reminder of the center of our universe.
First though,
Dzoti dodi.
    Wash with the medicine.
Some people stop to visit.
But I hear the Old People saying,
    "Wash first. Get clean. Then visit."
Dzoti, sitting behind Chiefs' Arbor.
    Medicine floating in the orange jug,
    resting on a faded wood bench.
Chiefs' Arbor looks good, nothing fallen. Yet.
    But spring storms will come before we dance.
Chief stands to the side of the *Dzoti,*
waiting with the old red-and-white porcelain dipper.
Buzz and I line up,
    facing east,
    looking toward the grounds.
        S'ae-sahn—clean ground, pure ground.
    Toward Gocho'o, Grampa Fire.
Dzoti dodi.
I stand behind Buzz.
    He with one pant leg always tucked in his boot.
    He turns and asks me to hold his hat and cane.
    I respond, "I don't need a cane."
        "You will," he laughs, and hands them to me.
Dzoti dodi.
Buzz finishes,
    shakes Chief's hand,
    takes his cap and cane.
    He wanders off to find his sister.
Now my turn,

just like last year.
And the year before that.
I take off my glasses,
hanging them in my back pocket,
Stuff my cap in the back of my jeans.
Cup my outstretched hands.
Chief gently dips in the medicine,
nudging the small sticks and twigs aside.
Pouring a little in my hands.
Cool.
Clear.
Cleansing.
I wash my hands, holding them out.
He pours again,
I wash my face.
Wash my hair.
Dzoti dodi.
Hold my hands out, waiting.
Chief carefully tips the dipper,
medicine falling in my cupped hands.
I sprinkle it on my shirt,
my jeans,
shaking the last drops on my boots.
Chief looks at me, questioning, silently,
the dipper three-quarters empty.
I hold my hands out again.
He pours.
Hold my hands over my shoulders, washing my back.
Now I nod to him,
he hands me the dipper,
cup first,
with its slight dents and chips.
You can see its age—but,
like us, it's still here.
I pause. Look at it,
then, to the east, to the grounds,
Toward Gocho'o, Grandfather,
white hair fading into the clay,
waiting for us.
Then I raise it and drink.

Thousands of years in one small sip.
Dzoti dodi,
    this year, every year.
I hand it back to Chief,
    then, finally, shake hands.
Now I am clean.
Now I can go onto the grounds.
    S'ae-sahn—clean ground, pure ground.
Year after year. Every year.
Dzoti dodi.

The Journey

Men, women, children, everyone, gathered and waiting. Almost time to move, to begin their journey.

They've done this before, now they will do it again.

The four chiefs checked on the people, making sure they were ready. That everything was ready.

"Are you coming with us?" a young boy asked Chief.

"No. You must do this for me."

"How will we know when to go?" another boy asked.

"You won't," Chief said.

The woman in front of the boys turned and smiled, "Watch us. When we go, you follow, we will all go together."

"How will you know when to go?" the little boys asked her.

Chief answered for her: "The leaders we have chosen will let them know it is time to go. That is their duty." With that, he and the other chiefs went. Watching. Seeing everyone was on the way.

The boys, like most young ones, were nervous and excited. But they did not know what lay ahead. The older woman knew what was behind them. The woman also knew what could happen. They knew tomorrow was only what might be, that could be exciting. But it could bring darkness.

The women waited.

Knowing this must be done. They would follow and help the others. That was their duty. To their families. To their relations.

Duty to those who had gone before and that would come after.

133

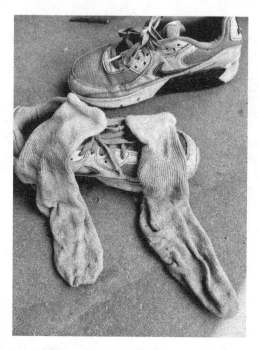

Stomp-dance shoes and sock, after a wet and rainy dance.

Chief finished talking to the people.

The two leaders in the front were ready. The leaders paused a moment. Praying maybe. Maybe just thinking. Then they began moving slowly forward.

Aganfa. Going to the east.

They thought about the things ahead. Looking. Thinking about all the people behind. They continued to the east, checking.

Finally, they reached the east, paused, and then returned to the people. Always looking, always thinking about what might come. And what they must leave behind.

When they returned, they paused upon seeing the people. Proud of their *Dzogala*, of their friends. Happy to see them again. The leaders turned around. Again, they went to the east, thinking of those who had gone before. Seeing what was ahead, they returned to the people.

Four times they did this. Just as the chiefs and old men had told them they must. The people waited for the leaders' return, anxious to begin their journey. When the leaders returned the fourth time, they paused, looking at the people.

Making sure everyone was ready.

Then the leaders whooped, signaling the people to follow them.

To the east. Men, women, children, old and young, all following along.

Moving no faster than the slowest among them.

The old and the young.

The chiefs and Old People had told stories of their other journeys.

Some hard. Some joyful. Some just were.

They were always instructed:

"*Hile ækuhna Hilea˘fene, Neh-yae hile anayana.*"

"Everyone come. Everyone move forward. Do not anyone fall back."

Just like the song.[3]

The two leaders moved steadily to the east.

Toward the sun, knowing everyone followed. When they reached the edge of the east, they turned.

Go-dan-fa, the north.

The cold.

And still the people followed.

Men, woman, children, old and young. Everyone following, everyone moving.

They came to the northern boundary, and again the leaders turned the people.

F'an-fa. To the west.

The direction the Old People, the Ancestors, went.

Some of the new Old People began to tire and moved slower. The leaders slowed the people, so they might continue together. They reached the western edge and turned again.

Wæ-fa. To the south.

Summer and the new year. The leaders encouraging the people, "*Nehakidana* (don't get lazy), do not fall back." The men and woman helping the old, keeping an eye on the young. Some of the people grew tired, but they remembered what the Old People told them: "Continue for those who went ahead so those yet to come can also continue."

The little boys were now grown men. Men who now encouraged the people. The old women were gone. Replaced by their daughters, granddaughters, and nieces.

"We are here. This is it," the leaders said, now themselves old men.

"Are we finished?" a little girl asked.

"No. You've just begun. This is yours now," Chief said.

Part 4

SHAJWANE AND FRIENDS

How Rabbit Gets His
Short Tail

This is one of the stories that I collected/recorded for our Euchee class in the early 1990s. Ida (Clinton) Riley was an old woman living in Bristow with her daughter who moved into a nursing home when her health declined. She was a marvelous storyteller, and the Euchee speakers in our class loved listening to the expressiveness she used in her native Euchee. As told and translated by Ida (Clinton) Riley, recorded by Greg Bigler.

Once there was a rabbit, and there was a wolf who wanted to be friends with this rabbit. Rabbit knew why, because Rabbit had lots of girlfriends that he went to play with often, whenever he got lonesome.

He didn't much want to be friends with Wolf, but he said, "If you want to be friends, we'll be friends."

Right away Wolf said, "Where do you go to have a good time, to play?"

"Well, I have some friends up here. I have some girlfriends up here I go play with."

Wolf said, "Well, let's go play with them."

So, they went to those girls' home. And oh, they played and played, and they were having a good time. But it wasn't too long till Wolf ran up and grabbed Rabbit by the arm and slung him into the corner and said, "When I was your size, I stayed home."

139

Oh, it hurt Rabbit's feelings so bad he didn't know what to do, he just didn't say anything. He took that, and thought maybe he just got (his feelings) too easily hurt. So he finally got up enough courage to get out and play again. He began playing again and just when he began having a good time again, Wolf went up and grabbed him by the arms and slung him into the corner and said, "When I was your size, I stayed home."

That time it hurt Rabbit so bad, and kind of made him sore, too, so he went on home. That evening he saw Wolf going home. So he went back up there and told his girlfriends, "Did you think that was some-one, that was a person you were playing with? That was my grand-father's horse, yes, that was my grandfather's horse." So he stayed and played with the girls till it got late and he went home.

Well, he knew Wolf would come later on to get him, so he kind of prepared. So, one day, he saw Wolf coming, and he made like he was real sick.

When Wolf came up and said, "We've got a score to settle. I want you to go to those girls' home and prove that I wasn't your grandfather's horse. You went and told them I was your grandfather's horse, and they wouldn't play with me."

So Rabbit said, "I don't see how I could tell them that when I've been here all this time since I left when we were down there together. I've been sick ever since then. But if you insist on me going, you will have to carry me—carry me on your back."

And Wolf agreed. So they made a bridle out of strings and put it over Wolf's face, and before they left, Rabbit got some spurs and put them in his pocket, and they left.

When they got close to the girls' house, Rabbit said, "I feel just a little bit better, if you don't mind, maybe you could trot just a little bit."

So Wolf trotted just a little bit as they went on. As they got close, Rab-bit said, "As we get into the yard, run, run along the fence, as I feel a lot better." So Wolf agreed.

When they got close to the house, well, Wolf started running along the fence, along the yard. (As they went, Rabbit slipped on those spurs and spurred Wolf.) And then Rabbit jumped off Wolf and hollered, "What did I tell you? I told you he was my grandfather's horse, didn't I!" And he started running, and Wolf running after him.

It just so happened there was a briar bush close to the girls' house, and Rabbit started to run under those blackberry bushes. As he started to run under them, Wolf was so close to Rabbit that he grabbed him by the tail and jerked Rabbit's tail off. And that's why Rabbit has a short tail.

Crane Visits Buffalo

One day as Crane finished his breakfast, he decided to visit Buffalo, whom he had not seen in a long time. Some thought it strange that Buffalo and Crane were such good friends. Crane was long, lean, and graceful, at least when he flew. Buffalo was large, solid, and steady. Crane, though, knew her as graceful and majestic. He loved to watch Buffalo and her relations as they moved together, as they danced across the land. So, Crane flew off to find his friend. She was standing, as usual, in front of her house smoking her tobacco in a small pipe. It reminded Crane of his youth when he would see the old women smoking their pipes. Buffalo called up to Crane as he flew toward her, admiring his graceful descent toward her house. She continued to puff on her pipe as he approached, pausing only to greet him, *"F'asahn, digadi!"*

As Crane settled in, Buffalo offered him tobacco, which, as always, he accepted but did not smoke. She watched him put it in his pouch.

"I never have seen you smoke," she remarked.

"And yet you always offer," he answered, "which I appreciate. You know smoking is bad for the voice."

"Yes, yes, it is," she admitted, "but no one wants to hear me sing, Brother Crane."

Buffalo paused a moment, thinking. She would sing if asked but had never felt comfortable singing. She would rather dance. On the other hand, she loved to hear Crane's voice. She knew many others who could sing, but Crane's songs were special. Perhaps that's why they were such good friends.

Crane must've been thinking the same thing, as he remarked, "And you dance so well. When you dance, the earth answers back. Sometimes even the tree frogs answer."

"My Grandmother used to tell how in the old days, when we were a great Buffalo Nation and all moved together, one could hear us dancing for miles and miles," Buffalo remarked. "When Grandmother told her stories, I could see those old ones moving and shaking. Stomp, stomp. Move, move. The joy they must have felt in being one people together," Buffalo thought out loud, sounding a bit sad, "Those days are gone."

Crane listened silently, nodding in agreement. Finally, he spoke, "That may be, my friend. Yet, you and I are still here. You still dance, and I still sing." Crane knew many looked at Buffalo and saw only her size, not thinking of her beauty, her movement to song. For all the grace Crane felt while flying, he felt awkwardness on the ground. His long legs just did not move in rhythm when he danced. In Crane and Buffalo's world, songs needed movement, dance, and dance needed song. So when the friends would visit, Crane would sing, and Buffalo would dance—each admiring the other, each finding joy in what they made together.

So they sang and danced. As the night went on, they sat and took a break. Buffalo asked, "I know you don't smoke, but don't I remember your father smoking? And he was a great singer."

Crane answered, "No, he never smoked." He paused for a moment, "I think you are remembering Uncle Crow. He smoked all the time. He started when he was in the war."

Buffalo thought that made sense. Crow liked to sing, and sing loudly, but no one really thought he sang well. Actually, Buffalo laughed, most would rather Crow not sing at all.

Crane continued, "My dad said Uncle Crow was a great warrior. In all the battles he went through, Uncle never got hit. He was one smart bird who knew how to move." Crane went on, "Uncle's children tried to get him to stop smoking. They told Uncle Crow it would kill him. They finally got him to stop, or so they thought. But my dad said Crow loved going to the casino, and he would find someone who was really smoking. Then Crow would sit right next to them, soaking up the smoke. His kids never figured it out."

Buffalo laughed at the story. She liked Crow. She liked most birds actually, which she told Crane.

"Well, thank you, sister!" Crane said.

"Well, most birds, except Buzzard, of course," Buffalo added.

Crane looked at her but didn't say anything.

"It's just creepy going out looking for something to eat and seeing Buzzard circling. Like he is just waiting for something bad to happen to us, so he can eat."

Crane agreed, "I know. Some of the others might clean up if something happens, but they don't follow you around hoping for an accident."

"Exactly. They are the ambulance-chasing lawyers of your bird world," she remarked.

"Yes, lawyers and Buzzard, birds of a feather so to speak," Crane said and they both giggled.

With that, Crane began singing "*Hoy-yoy Hey-yay*," and Buffalo started dancing, Shuffle, shuffle. Stomp, stomp. Like that they went through the night: Buffalo's great mane shaking and flowing back and forth; Crane's voice rising and falling—the two friends enjoying each other's gift.

Wolf Eats Tofu for Lunch

Wolf was sitting outside waiting for his friend Rabbit. Strangely, Wolf, unusually for him, felt a bit nervous. Wolf had asked his friend to bring him something, and Wolf hoped Rabbit had not told everyone. He wasn't quite ready for others to know about this, he just had to trust his friend's discretion. Which is why Wolf was nervous. Now he wished he'd treated his friend Rabbit nicer in the past. Oh, they were friends, but Wolf thought maybe he could have been a bit more considerate. Maybe Wolf had tried to overcompensate in the past, be too wolfish, as his friend would say. As Wolf thought, he remembered when he was a pup and his dad and uncles took him to hunt sheep, or sometimes his mom would take him. Occasionally, his cousins would join in, though they were older and more experienced. He loved the time they spent together. He always wanted to be just like them, all of them. They taught him how he should lie in wait, downwind, making sure it was safe. The stalking, just waiting there until the right moment, then sprint and leap on the prey. He got pretty good at it, very good actually, but the hunt itself was never satisfying. He never told anyone. All his relations were so proud of his skills, they wouldn't understand.

The emptiness didn't make much sense to him till he went away to college. Away from home, he met so many different animals, and not just to eat. His first class was "Eastern Philosophy for Predators." Wolf sat there and began to wonder why he had signed up for this, and then the professor came in and asked that same question of the class, "Why are you here?" Except, unlike Wolf, the professor had an answer.

144

"When you're out there stalking, lying in wait," the professor said, "as the minutes drag on, maybe for hours, you have two choices. You can just lie there, empty, bored. Or you can lie there, waiting and thinking. We are going to teach you the second option—to think."

After that, it all made sense to Wolf. He loved the class, reading about foreign religions and philosophies. He tried not to mention those topics back home. He doubted the pack would understand, how it was so like Wolf ways, how Vishnu's dancing, creating and continuing the world, was so like their own dances. The pack would just label him a citified wolf. Oh well. He felt he had begun to find what was missing in his life, understanding more of his own nature.

On his return home for spring and summer break, Wolf started thinking as he would lie in wait during the hunt. He wondered, why were sheep so docile? Why did wolves always eat sheep? Could wolves and sheep be friends? The sheep seemed so content except, of course, when he was leaping on them to get his teeth around their neck. Otherwise, they seemed pretty happy with life. Sheep always looked healthy, eating grass and vegetation. He did notice they never died of old age, but that really wasn't their fault, was it? Perhaps their diet was healthier? A lot of his relations were grumpy and had cardiac troubles. He looked at the grass and wondered if maybe he might like it. He tried a few blades, but spit them out. It really wasn't his thing, kinda grassy, but he decided to investigate more. After he got home, he looked on the internet and he saw that a plant-based diet led to a holistic, healthy lifestyle, or so the web claimed. Wolf thought maybe he would be happier with a vegetarian lifestyle. He knew he couldn't talk to any of his wolf relations about being a plant eater. They would never understand. That is when he thought of his friend Rabbit. Rabbit ate vegetarian, and if anyone was ever willing to talk about anything and everything, it was Rabbit. So off he went to find his friend.

After visiting with Rabbit and swearing Rabbit to secrecy, Wolf explained his thoughts. How he wanted to see if maybe he would be happier eating vegetarian, but he was worried about what his family would think. How he had no one else he could talk to about "being a plant muncher," as his relations derisively called them. Rabbit mulled it over for a while. He wondered about whether it was a good idea to help Wolf, being that Wolf was a wolf after all. But Rabbit decided if Wolf was serious, he would help, if Wolf trusted Rabbit and did as Rabbit told him. To start, he would bring some things over to Wolf's house to start his journey. Wolf reluctantly agreed, deciding he had to explore this side of himself. So, here Wolf was waiting for Rabbit. Finally, Rabbit came bouncing toward Wolf's house with a little sack slung over his shoulder.

Wolf could see Rabbit about to yell something, so he ran out and told him "*Huh'uhnle*, wait until we're inside, my friend!"

Once they were in the house, Rabbit laid out everything he brought: rice, some beautiful hot peppers, a few other ingredients, and something he called tofu.

"It's kind of plain looking. And not much smell," Wolf said looking down his long nose at the tofu.

"Well, yes. But it's very healthy for you, a superfood," Rabbit said. "It may be bland, but it's what we put with tofu that makes it magic. Aren't you are always telling me about the Asian courses you took in college? Explaining to me how you love Chinese brush painting, which captured my cousin the hare in a few simple brush strokes, how it's the art of the bland?"

They both started laughing at that, though Rabbit's laugh turned nervous and then stopped quickly when Rabbit noticed Wolf's teeth as Wolf laughed. Even if Wolf might want to eat vegetarian now, Rabbit still felt uneasy. Those fangs just gleamed a bit much for Rabbit's liking, friend or not.

Finally, they got to fixing lunch, Rabbit telling Wolf how to prepare everything, chopping, mixing, cooking, steaming the rice. After they had everything ready, they sat down to eat. It looked pretty, Wolf had to admit, and he was surprised how much he liked the tofu. Right then, he realized this was what was missing in his life, what he wanted. His family might not understand, but tofu tasted good, he felt whole. He thought he could finally embrace a side he had been denying.

"A vegetarian wolf," Wolf said out loud, and Rabbit and Wolf both started laughing. After that, Rabbit didn't worry about Wolf's teeth. And that is how Wolf had tofu for lunch.

Pray for Us

It was late when Rabbit got home. His wife had fixed supper and waited for him, for a while. However, she eventually got tired and hungry, and a bit mad, and had already eaten by the time he got home. She assumed he was up to his usual antics, which, of course, he had been. However, once he was home and it was just him and his wife, most of that dropped away. His behavior was not an act, it was his nature. It was, however, not his only nature. It was just the side that most knew and talked about, the one they wanted to see. Rabbit asked his wife how her day was, showing genuine interest. That side of him is why she put up with Rabbit all these years, despite his other "behavior," as she put it to her friends. At home, with just his wife, he could let that other side go, for the most part, and relax. His wife told him to sit down and she would bring him dinner. She got his plate and set it in front of him. He thanked her as she sat to be with him.

After he had eaten a bit, she asked him, "And how was your day?" He told her some of what he did, the things that happened to him. She shook her head, asking him, "Why do you still do those things, Rabbit?" He raised his head from his food and looked questioningly at her. She said, "I know, I know. But, still, why?"

Rabbit shrugged and said, "It's what I do." Rabbit's wife thought to herself, "His adventures were more lovable when I was young." But, here she was, all these years later. Their life together was good, overall. Especially with so much change all around them. Sister Buffalo and her husband were long divorced. And Robin was, what, on his third wife??

147

She could understand that with Robin, though, as he was good to look at, and what a voice. But, Robin was lazy, and that would get tiring after a while. Rabbit and his wife sometimes talked, or gossiped, when it was just the two of them, of friends who were changed or gone. She suspected Rabbit wasn't really doing all the things he used to do either, though he would never admit it. She should be happy about that, but it sometimes worried her, too.

So it was that they were sitting there at the table, Rabbit finishing his dinner. Sitting there, neither saying anything for now. Like a couple that had been together a very long time, which they had after all. When he was done, she got up and quietly cleared the table. As she wiped the table (Rabbit was always so messy), they heard a knock at the door. For a moment neither moved. It had been a long time since they'd had a visitor, maybe since Bear came over. Rabbit got up, went to the door, and opened it. *Nehgoahn.* No one was there. Rabbit stepped outside to look around, but no one was in sight. Rabbit took one more look around, then, slightly annoyed, went back inside and closed the door. Halfway back to the table, he again heard a knock. Again, a bit more annoyed, he went to the door. *Depuhle, nehgoahn.* Again, there was no one there. This time, Rabbit paused and listened. It was dusk now, and Rabbit remembered his grandmother telling him this was a special time of day, when things happened, to pay attention. Of course, his grandmother had said that about all kinds of times of the day: early morning right after sunup, the moment just before first light, straight-up noon, midnight. Actually, just about any time of day was special according to her, as Rabbit recalled. But it was dusk now, so this was the special moment Rabbit remembered Golaha Shajwane (Grandmother Rabbit) talking about. So, he paused quietly. Waiting in the doorway. Now he could remember hearing Golaha Shajwane saying, "Don't stand in the doorway. Doorways are for things to go through." Rabbit wondered to himself, "Why are there so many rules?" But he stepped aside, and as he did so, he felt a voice ask, "Can I come in?"

Rabbit responded, *"Huhn. Aheguhn"* (Yes, come in). After a moment, Rabbit closed the door and went to the table. His wife stuck her head in from the kitchen, inquisitively. He asked his wife to get their visitor a coffee. She looked around, but paused only a moment, and with a shrug got two coffees and put one in front of Rabbit and the other across from her husband. Then she went about her chores but kept her ears open, listening. Rabbit sat patiently waiting. He began to notice, out of the corner of his eyes, when he was not looking, an indistinct form, a shape, sitting by the coffee.

They sat there quietly for a while. Rabbit wasn't sure what to do next. Finally, he decided this was a guest after all, so he would show the respect due any guest and asked: "*Sahngaahnle? Neh'yahuhnle?*" Are you hungry? Rabbit nodded to his wife, who went to the kitchen. She looked at the leftovers from supper, and wondered to herself, "Do Spirits like Rabbit's food?" She shrugged and decided that this evening they would. She remembered how her mother had instructed her to prepare a meal for a Spirit. "We offer what we have," was what she was taught. She found a small plate, put a little of each food she had prepared on it and brought it out. She was going to get a cup of water, but, as she had already brought coffee, thought maybe that was enough. Then she went back to cleaning up the kitchen.

Soon enough the Spirit answered, "I have been good. Thank you. The ceremonies of my people are finished for the year, they had good participation. I am lucky. My people, the ones I am tied to, they still try to do what they were taught. Sometimes, I step back and look down at them as they are carrying out their ceremonies. The dances are so beautiful, it fills me with happiness to see. Gohahtine blessed me with these people. I am very proud. It will, I think, hold me for another year. What more could a Spirit ask?"

Rabbit nodded, agreeing, "Those people, those Indians, like yours, are the same ones who will tell my stories." Rabbit went on, "I used to love hearing the mothers telling their children stories about me and Bear, Wolf, Crane, my friends, and the others. I could hear mothers with their children, at night, quietly telling them our tales, filling the children with wonder, history, and love. Those days were the best."

Spirit seemed to nod in agreement, then asked how Rabbit was doing now. Rabbit said, "Fine." The Spirit said nothing in response, so Rabbit continued, "Well, things have been—slow." His visitor seemed to agree. Or at least Rabbit thought it agreed. Rabbit wondered, was "it" an "it," or how was he to refer to his visitor? Oh well, he would just go with what he knew. Rabbit added, "There seem to be changes all about us. Like summer changes to fall, except we are the changes."

Rabbit's visitor agreed. "It is that way for us, too. Our worlds are getting smaller. And some of my relations and friends are not doing well. Just like you," his visitor continued, "fewer people feeding us, taking care of us."

That struck a nerve with Rabbit. "I know!" Rabbit said animatedly, "no one even talks about me anymore!!" His visitor looked at Rabbit, and Rabbit added, "Well, not like they used to, only sometimes. There are a few young people learning about my heroics . . . but, so many of my best adventures are ignored." Rabbit's wife, hearing her husband getting excited, looked into the room, and then came in and sat down, listening. His visitor waited.

Rabbit continued, not really paying attention to the other two. "But, Coyote! Oh, everyone talks about Coyote. Coyote this, Coyote did that. Did Coyote save everyone from Gojithlah?" By now, Rabbit was up and pacing back and forth. "No! I did!" Rabbit exclaimed, "Coyote even has movies about him! He's not even that cute," Rabbit said crossly. With that, Rabbit noticed his wife staring at him with that look that all wives give when they've heard the same thing from their husband for the last hundred years. Rabbit, feeling a bit embarrassed, calmed down. He took his seat again, knowing his visitor must have come for a reason. By way of apology, as much as he ever could, Rabbit said, "Sometimes my nature runs a bit strong, my friend."

Spirit laughed and said, "We must each be what we are." Then Spirit continued, "but that does not mean we do not get tired. For us, some of us, the lucky ones, we still have people who are strong in their ways. Those Spirits whose people continue to do the things they are supposed to. Other Spirits, though, their people are fewer." Spirit had Rabbit's attention now as Spirit continued, "In your case, maybe people no longer tell your sagas. For us, maybe people don't carry on our ceremonies. Some few of us don't even have people over on that side, they have all disappeared. Think of those people who have disappeared. There is no one left. Those Spirits are alone over here."

Rabbit paused; he had never thought about things in these terms before. Rabbit and his wife both felt sad for their new friend, and their friend's relations. The two of them sat waiting, sensing Spirit had more to say. "I have some Spirit relations who are in museums, some taken far away, overseas to museums. You know some of us are tied to bundles, to medicines, to drums, or such," his friend said.

Rabbit nodded, he knew about those things, he had grown up around medicines. Despite everything, he tried to be careful and respectful of such things. Tried to be at least, he sheepishly admitted. His visitor continued, "As I said, many of the ones in the museums, they are locked up or stranded, or both, they have no one anymore. No offerings. No clothes made to replace the worn-out ones. No little meals. No tobacco.

No ceremonies. No one who knows how they are to be taken care of. No prayers."

The longer Rabbit and his wife listened, the sadder they became, knowing their friend experienced the same loss Rabbit and his friends suffered. Rabbit, sensing Spirit wanted more than coffee, asked, "Well, I am not sure what I can do. Is there something you want of me?"

Spirit took a while to answer. "*Huhn.* Shajwane, I know who you are, and what you are." Rabbit accepted this statement. He glanced at his wife. She looked at him, both thinking that she was always saying the same thing to Rabbit. Spirit continued, "But I also know you understand. So, when you say your prayers, offer your tobacco, when you ask for blessings, I ask a favor. Say a prayer for us."

Then their visitor added, "We need your prayers, too."

Rabbit simply agreed: "*Ahe dilehuhn.*"

With that, Spirit departed.

Winter Solstice—A Modern Di'ile

W hen we are all together, sometimes we would tell how Shajwane (Rabbit) loved winter. Shajwane always looked forward to summer ceremonies, Green Corn—the Indians' New Year—and all the dances. But winter, with its solstice, the winter holidays, always felt special. The short days, long nights, the cool, cold weather with the first snow layering the world. The earth sleeping and recovering. For Rabbit, it meant a time for staying in, visiting with friends, telling stories, and of course, sharing food. Some of his friends always missed out on the winter festivities. Bear slept most of the winter; Crane, Cardinal, and Goose flew south. And Shajwane never did know where Turtle went during the winter. But the others who stayed kept those who were absent in their thoughts, praying for a safe return come spring, in time for the start of the ceremonial season.

Now, in the short days and cold nights, it was time for the winter holidays. In preparation, Shajwane was making the last-minute trips to Walmart when he ran into Wolf. They stopped, each leaning on their carts, both explaining that the wives had sent them to get a few items each forgot the last time they were here, earlier in the day. Rabbit liked the opportunity to be out, but he could tell the crowds did not sit well with brother Wolf.

Shajwane asked him, "*Sahngaahnla?* (How have you been?) It has been a few months since I saw you."

"*Huhn.* It has been a while," Wolf agreed, "I've been okay. I love the winter, the solstice and the holidays. I love putting on my winter coat, so warm and full. Getting out in the cold, the snow. Last week, I was glad for the coat, with that cold and wind biting like a paper cut."

Rabbit nodded, adding, "But this week. What happened? I'm sweating, it has been so warm, I feel like I am at a stomp in July. Hot, sweaty but with no hickory smoke to cover my scent."

Wolf laughed, "*Huhn!* I could smell you three aisles over, my friend. It has been this way more and more in recent years. I wonder how Sage (Bear) sleeps. And I heard Crane talking about not even going south."

Shajwane just shook his head in agreement.

Wolf continued, "For all the stories they tell about you causing trouble, they can't blame you for these warmer winters, *Dzogala*."

"I know," Rabbit agreed, though he was not sure that was really a compliment. "It makes me mad. And I have heard it will not get any better. They talk about me like I'm a troublemaker. But did I do this? No. Yet here I am, trying to decide, Is it cold out today? Do I get out my coat? Is it hot? Do I open the window? It is so confusing." They were both quiet for a moment, thinking. Then, Rabbit said, "Well, *doandaehnlaehn*, I need to finish here before the wife wonders what I'm up to. She's always so suspicious."

Wolf looked at Shajwane and laughed, "Right. Why would she ever wonder about you?"

Rabbit saw Wolf's grin, and hurriedly continued, "Anyway, I need to make sure I don't forget something. Again. You and the family coming over tonight?"

"*Huhn*," Wolf answered, turning to things they could control. We will be over." With that, they fist-pawed and were on their way.

Later that night, as the moonlight fell on the snow-covered houses and fields, Wolf, Shajwane, and the others gathered to celebrate the holidays. They shared food and stories, remembering too many friends no longer with them. For now, the warmth of family and friends, and not the weather, filled the air. Late into the evening, their laughter, the smell of food, and fellowship flowed out of Rabbit's home, out to the fields, settling on the earth, marking this spot with their memories, reminding the winter they were still here.

Shajwane, Wolf, and all their friends wish each of you a Merry Winter Solstice and Happy Holidays.

Shajwane Gets Served

Shajwane (Rabbit) liked going to dances and ceremonies. Those things taught one right from wrong, which in part helped him to usually do the right thing. Not always for the right reason, but occasionally even for the right reason. This wasn't one of those times.

Shajwane knew some things and pretended to know much more. Because of that, some would ask for his help. Maybe finding medicines, or maybe offering prayers when in particular need. Rabbit's friends like Bear and Crane would shake their heads at those moments but wouldn't say anything, as it was not their place. Later, they might check with Rabbit to "see how it went." Rabbit would tell everyone all about what he did and how thankful the other animals were. Occasionally, though, Rabbit wouldn't give a direct answer to Bear or Crane. Then Rabbit's friends knew he had not yet done what he was supposed to do. Or that it had not gone as planned. After this happened a few times, Crane decided to say something to his friend.

"Did you offer those prayers?" Crane began.

Rabbit was silent, looking away.

"When one learns a thing, you commit to doing it whenever you are asked," Crane continued.

"I know that," Shajwane responded.

"Well, I'm happy to hear you say so. But, if you continue this way, something is going to happen, my friend," Crane said. "That's what the old ones said."

"I know," Shajwane repeated, somewhat crossly, "I know what to do, don't worry so much!"

"*Huhn,*" was all Crane said, and then went on his way.

Not too long afterward, a woman sought out Rabbit, asking for his help. Lately, she had been thinking of her mother, who had passed away the year before. Now she noticed a few odd things happening around her house. She decided she needed to do something about these things but didn't know what.

Shajwane listened politely and looked very attentive. Finally, he said yes, he could help, he just needed tobacco to pray with. The woman had expected that and brought along some plug tobacco. She gave it to Rabbit, thanked him for his help, and told him how lucky we were to have him, and then went on her way. Rabbit felt very important getting asked to do this for the woman. He decided tomorrow at sunrise would be the right time to carry out the request. The rest of the day he went around telling anyone he met he had an important thing to do tomorrow. Shajwane was so busy impressing everyone, he didn't notice how late it was getting. When he realized the sun had set, he hurried home to bed.

The next day, he woke up early, before the sun came up. He decided he could rest a bit longer and went back to sleep. When he woke again, it was midmorning, and the sun was well on her journey for the day. Rabbit, looking at the sky, thought to himself, "Well, it is so late, tomorrow I will do as the woman asked me." Then, he went about his chores for the rest of the day. But the same thing happened the next morning, with him oversleeping. Rabbit was feeling bad about this for a bit, but he got over it. As he went about his business, he realized he was out of tobacco for himself, and the store was closed for the weekend. Then he remembered the plug tobacco the woman had given him. He thought, "I can just use that and replace it when the store opens." Of course, the same thing happened the next day, and the next. After a while, Rabbit forgot his promise and obligations, and even forgot about replacing the tobacco he borrowed.

However, someone, or something, had not forgotten. One day, as Shajwane was talking with some girls, Wolf came up to him.

"Shajwane? Mr. Rabbit?" he asked.

"Yes, that's me, can I help you, sir?" Shajwane answered.

With that, Wolf handed Rabbit some papers and said, "You've been served."

Rabbit looked down at the papers, which began:

"You have been sued for conversion. Having agreed to provide tobacco to certain Unnamed Spirits, and having received said tobacco to do so, you did willfully and wrongfully withhold said tobacco from the above Unnamed Spirits. Having failed to do as you committed, you are commanded to appear Four Days hence to answer said Unknown Spirits as to how you intend to fulfill said duties and determine damages."

The summons concluded: "Failure to comply with this summons will result in further action taken without notice."

Shajwane began to shake as he read the summons. He remembered his grandfather telling him how much trouble angry Spirits could cause. He wasn't sure what he should do. He was so worried and scared about it he started to cry. Then he started sobbing. Finally, thinking about it, he decided he would speak with his friend Crane. Crane always seemed to know about these types of things. Shajwane found Crane and handed him the papers. Crane got his glasses out and read the summons. Then he looked at Rabbit and back at the papers and then back at Rabbit. He had Rabbit tell him the whole story of what had happened. When Rabbit finished, Crane took off his glasses and put them away, and sat there quietly for a long time. Finally, he spoke to Rabbit.

"Well, it is always bad when you agree to do things for Spirits and then fail to follow through. Remember your *golaha* (grandmother) telling how she was too tired to put tobacco out when the Thunders came through?"

Rabbit looked scared and nodded his head. His *golaha,* a little old full-blood rabbit, told how one night a storm came through and brought the Thunders. They were rumbling, bringing the rains and their blessings. But she was too tired to get out of bed to feed the Thunders. Later that night, the Thunders shook the house and made her favorite dishes fall and break. From then on, she made sure everyone took care of the Thunders whenever she heard the storms come around.

Crane continued, "When you agreed to this, you had a duty. More importantly, the Spirits had a right for you to follow through and bring them their tobacco. They were expecting it. And now, now you just used it up for yourself." And Crane stood there shaking his head muttering, "This is not good, not good at all."

Rabbit could barely breathe by this time. "What can I do?" he whimpered.

"Well, I have a couple of things you can do between now and then, and then when you appear in four days. Maybe that will help. Maybe not. But if I tell you, you must do them. No fooling around this time."

Looking very subdued, Shajwane said, "*Huhn,*" agreeing. With that, Crane told Rabbit what to do for the next four days, every day. No excuses.

Rabbit, being Rabbit, was tempted not to follow through, but each time he thought about it, he felt someone watching him, so he did as Crane directed.

Finally, the day arrived when Rabbit was to appear in court. Rabbit got up, washed his face, completed the last task as Crane directed, had a cup of coffee, got himself ready, and hurried on his way to court.

And this is where my telling of Rabbit's story ends. For now. Stories such as this about Rabbit, Crane, Spirits, and lawsuits depend not only on the storyteller but also on the listener. The story depends on the telling and the listening. We are in the story together. I do not know how it ends, and I may never know. Shajwane clearly did not do what he was supposed to, but he tried to make amends, eventually doing as he was told. In our world, in our understanding, we, just as Shajwane, have duties to these Spirits and medicines, to these things we have been given. Those ways we have been told to continue. It is a covenant. Like Shajwane giving the tobacco. When he was sued, perhaps the duty of Rabbit to do as he was asked is a reflection, a mirror to the Spirit's right to the tobacco. Duty and Right. Tying each other together. If Unknown Spirit has a right to the tobacco, then they get to sue poor Rabbit. I don't know how that works. Perhaps it is different for your people, or for your family. Until we understand, poor Rabbit will live in limbo, or perhaps in purgatory, to borrow from our Christian friends. You are free to decide for yourself. Perhaps your traditions, your ways, your Old People, would dictate a different decision in Unknown Spirit versus Rabbit. *That is okay. I will let you finish the story. However, as long as we do what we said we would, then none of us need to end up like Shajwane, awaiting court.*

Part 5

❧

FINAL MATTERS

Little Man Makes a Jailbreak

The other day Jackson's wife, Mary, asked him, again, if he finally got that old truck of his running. He had that thing forever, usually sitting in the back being worked on. He would never sell it, though, and Mary would ask him about it occasionally, not expecting a good answer.

"Not yet," he said, "but I got the parts yesterday."

"Well, I was wondering," Mary said. "I knew you went to get them, but when you were gone all day, I thought maybe you couldn't find them."

"No," he answered, "I ran into nephew and got to visiting."

"Your sister's boy?" she asked.

"Yes."

"How is he?" she asked.

"Well, pretty good, but his youth is catching up to him," Jackson laughed.

"Not the old warrants again?" Jackson's wife said, looking worried, "I told him he needed to take care of those things, or it would be trouble. His mom was always getting on him about that."

"No. Not warrants," Jackson laughed. "Not this time. He can deal with those."

"Then what?"

"It's his boy."

Jackson's wife looked concerned. She always had a soft spot for Jackson's nephew. He was basically a good young man. Hard-working and always at the dances and the work parties when Chief called. But he had a wild streak when he was younger. He gave his mom a lot of worries with his drinking and running around, mainly when he was at ball tournaments, and he was always at ball tournaments. He had been a really good athlete and should have gone to school on a scholarship but didn't want to leave home. He went to Haskell for a semester or two and that was it. Then he bounced around for a while, till about six or seven years ago when he met a girl from one of the other grounds. She was a bit younger. Jackson and Mary would laugh and tell each other she was probably the only one not related to him. Nephew's wife was a good woman with a good head on her shoulders. But she definitely wouldn't put up with nephew's crap. Nephew settled down, stayed sober, and now they had two beautiful little kids. A boy about five and a girl about three.

So now Jackson's wife worried something was wrong between them.

"No, no," Jackson said, "not like that . . ."

She looked at him, waiting.

"Well, you know Little Man started kindergarten last week," Jackson began.

She nodded, remembering he was at that age.

"Anyway, they took him to the meet and greet at school," Jackson said, "and Little Man seemed really excited about school. He liked his teachers, saw his cousins in the other classes, got his new clothes and a backpack from Indian Education. Nephew was pretty proud. All set to go. Then they took him to the first day of class. Mom and Dad were trying to leave, but I guess the kid didn't realize they were going to leave him and he would be on his own with just the other children and the teacher. He had a fit. Screaming and crying, like that. Nephew said he wanted to beat his butt, but with everyone looking on, he didn't know what to do. And his wife was trying to mother him to death. So, finally, Nephew and his wife just left."

"Well, they always spoil that little boy," Jackson's wife said, shaking her head. "A good kid but tied to Momma's apron strings."

"Payback for the trouble Nephew caused his mama," Jackson said, nodding, "and it gets better."

"Okay. What?" she asked.

Jackson went on to explain that after they left, Little Man seemed to settle down, and it seemed like everything was good. Seemed. Apparently, he was just waiting for his moment. When the teacher turned her attention to the other children, he took off.

"Took off?" she asked.

"Yes, like a bolt of lightning," Jackson said. "Out of the room, down the hall, past the principal, Mr. Johnson. Remember him?"

His wife nodded.

"Past him and out the door," Jackson continued. "Mr. Johnson was surprised and took a moment before he could react, and that was all it took. Little Man was out the door, flying toward freedom."

His wife looked at Jackson again, drinking her coffee, waiting for the rest.

"Well, Mr. Johnson is still in pretty good shape," he explained, "coaching kids all those years, so he turned, and he took off running after him. Nephew said Mr. Johnson caught Little Man but not before he was halfway up the fence behind the school."

Jackson's wife didn't want to, but she couldn't help laughing, thinking of Little Man making a jailbreak. Reminding her of those old stories of Doc Johnson, the old Indian doctor who used to get picked up for drinking back in the twenties, all the elders saying white man jails could never hold him, for some reason. "At least Little Man didn't have to turn into an owl to escape," she said.

"Nephew had to come back to school, of course," Jackson continued, "and he got all over his boy. Finally, the boy went back to class, and I guess things finally calmed down. Guess Little Man just decided to give it his best shot, and that was good enough."

"Did Little Man or Nephew get in any trouble for it?" Mary asked.

"Well, they got into less trouble than when Nephew used to pull that stuff back when he was in school," Jackson said. "Or when I was in school for that matter," Jackson added with a smile. "The only thing was, as Nephew was leaving Mr. Johnson's office afterward, Mr. Johnson told Nephew to wait a minute, and closed the door. Nephew thought, okay, now we're going to hear it. But Mr. Johnson just looked at Nephew, and said, 'Damn, your boy is fast! You be sure and sign him up for our league next month, okay?' Nephew said that he would. Then they shook hands, and Nephew left. Anyway, that's what took so long yesterday."

"Well, I'm not surprised," his wife said.

"Wait till his little girl gets to her teens, then Nephew is going to have trouble," Jackson said.

"Yes, he will," Jackson's wife said, smiling, and asked, "So, when are you going to get that truck of yours running?"

Jackson's Friend Takes a Road Trip

Jackson had to go to the city, over to the university to see an old friend who taught there. His friend wanted to visit about something. Jackson hadn't asked about what, as it didn't matter to him. He figured it was a nice chance to catch up with his friend. Probably about a class he was teaching, maybe something to do with one of the tribes, or could be something else. The Professor, as Jackson called him, often called to talk about ceremonies and dances and Old People they had known. His friend was from one of the western tribes, a pow-wow Indian, as Jackson would tell him. Jackson didn't have anything bad to say about pow-wows or his friends who traveled that circuit, it just wasn't Jackson's ways, at least not nowadays. He had run around the pow-wow circuit when he was young, but it had been a few years ago—to be honest, getting to be a lot of years ago. The Professor didn't mind. He knew Jackson's commitment to his ways and admired anyone who tried to follow what they had been told and learned, especially as well as Jackson did. The Professor met a lot of people who talked about traditions. His friend Jackson, though, didn't talk about them much unless he knew you and you asked. But if asked, he had a lot of insight, though it might take him a while to get around to the point. Like their adventures when they were young, his stories wandered around awhile. But, eventually, they got to where they were going.

The Professor was a couple of years younger than Jackson, but the two of them used to run together quite a bit when they were still in their twenties, going to pow-wows, running after girls, visiting places and

Shajwane in truck. Illustration by Adam Youngbear.

people. They never got into real trouble, but, as they reminded each other occasionally, they did kind of stare at it a few times. They both had a streak back then that they let out together. Each had been in the service, but not together. He knew Jackson had served overseas, but Jackson never talked about it, didn't even mention it. For the Professor, it was a big part of his life being part of his tribe's traditional military and veterans' societies, where he was well respected for his service.

When Jackson told his wife that the next afternoon he was going over to the university, he didn't have to explain anything else to her. Not after forty-plus years together. She just looked at him for a moment and asked, "You going to take that old truck of yours? Will it make it there and back? Are you sure?" She knew it would, but that was her job to look out for him.

Jackson didn't say anything. He knew she liked that old truck, but she would never admit it.

"Are you going to take that old man you been talking to?" she asked next. "Maybe he would like to get out."

At that, Jackson looked at her and said, "What old man?" He didn't think anyone knew anything about his friend, let alone could see or hear him. Mary rolled her eyes and shook her head, waiting.

"I don't know, I guess if he wants," Jackson finally answered. "I hadn't thought about him traveling."

"Well, you take your tobacco everywhere, why not him, too?"

He had visited with the Old Man a few times and felt his presence other times, almost feeling comfortable about it now. If one could ever find such a thing normal. His wife must have noticed the extra coffee, or cigarettes. Or maybe she saw him, too. He no longer was surprised at what she knew, that habit of her knowing things had been the end of a lot of fun for their kids when their kids were growing up. Thinking about it, Jackson had no response, so he just said, "*Huhn.* Maybe."

That evening Jackson went out back and started a fire, bringing extra coffee, a cup, and cigarettes, setting them down on the far chair. After a bit he said, to no one in particular, "Tomorrow, I am going to see an old friend, one of those pow-wow Indians who teaches. I'll probably take the old roads over there, should be a nice drive. And he always has some interesting stories. Just be me going, unless someone wanted to ride along." Then he added, as an afterthought, "If someone can do such things." He felt strange saying it out loud, but he knew his wife would know if he didn't. Besides, what did he know? What rules applied to traveling for his friend? At least he was polite and invited him. Hopefully, he thought to himself, this road-trip buddy wouldn't get them arrested like the Professor did in the old days.

The next day, a bit past noon, he headed out, grabbing two coffees, placing one on each side of the console. It was about a forty-minute drive to the city. He could have saved fifteen or twenty minutes if he took the interstate, but he liked the old roads, the roads he took when he was young and running around. He used to say he could go all the way to Oklahoma City, traveling across blacktop only twenty-four feet at a time, sticking to the dirt roads. The Highway Patrol didn't travel those dirt roads, and County tended to leave you alone on them. Tended to, he laughed to himself, remembering. Jackson had a lot of stories from those days.

Thinking that his friend might have come along, he decided to speak his memories aloud. He thought it a good thing regardless, as voicing one's memories gave life to them. Jackson was usually a quiet man, but he could tell a story when the mood hit, and he thought to himself what his wife said. He thought his friend might be along, he didn't know how these things worked after all.

He began by saying how he had more fun telling these stories than actually living them. He felt lucky, was lucky, to be alive. He and the Professor had more than a few friends who didn't make it. Drinking or drugs, fights, a couple just disappeared. It was exciting when you are twenty-one, but it got old when you are thirty running around, drinking. No real home or settled family. At forty, people would start talking about how sad it was, how you looked old, tired, that you used to have so much potential. By the time those people were fifty, they were dead, gone. Jackson talked about how that happened to too many friends. It happened to his cousins, he said, and he was watching it happen to some of his nephews, and worse to a niece or two. He talked about that as he drove past the old places he used to see, the Old People who had welcomed them.

Jackson's people gave life to these places. Jackson wondered aloud what had happened to the Old Man's friends who had been of these places. He talked about how down that old road had been those two old sisters who made corn flour the old way. His mom loved that stuff, had some stories about when she and her siblings had to make it at their grandma's place. Jackson said the sisters' names, the Madison girls, that's what everyone called them. They were in their seventies when he met them some forty or fifty years ago. But once you got a name, that followed you forever. It was actually a sign of respect, Jackson thought, it placed you with your people. The Madison girls, Jackson thought out loud.

At a funeral some twenty years back, Jackson's speaker from the grounds was talking about the man, Jackson's age, who had passed away. His speaker at the time was a generation older than Jackson, a World War II vet, and sitting next to Jackson out back by the medicine for after the funeral. He told Jackson, "I didn't know his first name was Robert," speaking of the man who died. "I always thought it was Byrd with a "y." Forty years, and I thought it was Byrd, not "Bird" with an "i." After a bit, his speaker asked, "Did you know that Bird was just his nickname? The obituary said his real name was Robert. I knew his Indian name, but I guess I never knew his white man name." Jackson laughed at the memory. His old speaker was sitting there with the ever-present cigarette between his fingers, him daring the long ash to fall off the cigarette. Even after his heart attack, he smoked. That old speaker was tough. Jackson knew he'd been one of those who island-hopped in all the Pacific battles, but he never, ever spoke about it. Funny, too, nasty sometimes, especially late at night when the young men were getting tired. He'd get done leading, coming back to take his place in the arbor and ask the boys, "How'd like it, baby??" and then laugh. But he could sing those old songs, and old stories, too. Sometimes he'd sing and only the old chief knew how to answer it. Jackson told the old speaker, he was just making them up, to which he would laugh and say, "I might be." Jackson remembered him one Green Corn dancing all day, dancing all night till sunup, then when we were all done, telling us he had to do a shift at the factory at 9:00 A.M. Later we asked him how that

went, and he said they were shorthanded, so he pulled a double shift
that day. He smoked to the day he died in his nineties. He said if the
Japanese didn't kill me, don't guess smoking will. Tough, that is what
those old men and women were, Jackson said.

As Jackson thought about these places, he continued speaking, telling his stories. He felt good saying them aloud, bringing them to life.
Maybe his friend was there, maybe not, he didn't think it mattered.
Either way, it felt right to breathe the stories. Indians shouldn't forget
their Old People and old places. That was what his uncle used to tell
him. A man should know these things, as Uncle would say.

So, he drove past the road that led to the Madison girls' place, past
the roads to the old allotments, and past the turnoff to the grounds,
telling stories. He eventually got on the highway to the university. From
there it didn't take long till he was at the college, where he found a spot,
parked his truck, and walked toward his friend's office, seeing all the
earnest-looking young people, mostly white, he noticed, and a few
others. He didn't see any Indians, he said to himself, though nowadays
one couldn't always tell—some Indians were light skinned, and he had
some fair-haired nephews and nieces who were strong members at the
grounds. He said out loud, in Euchee, just in case, "Some of my own
relations aren't much Indian by blood. But if they take medicine and
are still there at sunup Sunday morning after Green Corn, they're
Indian to me," hoping if his friend was along he would agree.

Anyway, Jackson thought, it was a beautiful campus, tree-lined with
plants and flowers and brick buildings. Those old redbrick buildings.
He didn't know how old really, but they looked like the ones he saw in
the pictures of colleges. When he visited the Professor, he sometimes
wished he'd gone to school. Jackson enjoyed learning, he thought learning was a lot like listening to stories, and this looked like a place full of
knowledge and opportunities to learn, to understand things. Of course,
he felt that way when he was in the woods, too. Looking at the professors wandering by, he guessed no one could really fill up on either kind
of knowledge. Though, speaking out loud, he imagined there were more
than a few learned fools here, too. So much knowledge and things to
know, curiosity was something one should never give up. He assumed
that, like himself, they had spent a lifetime trying to understand. Speaking his thoughts, he wondered how many of these academics realized
how much there was still there in the elders. A lot of his own people
didn't realize how much was out there. Or how close we are to losing it,
no matter what they claimed. Shortly, he found the Professor's office

JACKSON'S FRIEND TAKES A ROAD TRIP

and went in. There were books piled on his friend's shelves all around his tight little office. Tribal stuff, history books about Indians, with tribal artifacts stuck here and there. It looked like some cross between a library and an elder's house all tossed together, like some kind of a half-made quilt.

His friend was happy to see Jackson. He didn't get to visit about Indian stuff as much as he used to. Too busy teaching white people about Indians, as he put it. They sat and visited in the little office, remembering their time running around, talking about family and what they had coming up. After about an hour, the Professor told Jackson, "Let's go get some coffee." Jackson was always good with that of course. He had been there before, so he knew the coffee was just across the way from his friend's office. The cafeteria had a nice outside patio where they could sit and visit. As they went, his friend finally got around to what Jackson assumed was his reason for asking Jackson to visit.

"I have a student who might be a distant relation of yours, or at least of your people. He seems pretty smart, dedicated, and very into activism."

"But?" Jackson said, looking at his friend.

"Exactly," his friend laughed.

The young man the Professor mentioned had not been around his own people much, had mostly gained his knowledge through books and perhaps other Indians. He was involved in activism around campus but not one who had actually been out to the old places. He didn't know his people. Jackson's friend hoped that perhaps he might start making some connections, that it would be good for him.

"We aren't here forever," the Professor said, something the two of them repeated a lot when they were younger, raising hell.

"Maybe you aren't, but I intend to be—*shah!*" Jackson answered, then continued, "I realize my age more and more every day I try to get up. Okay, sure, where is he?"

"I'll text him. He'll be here in a bit." He explained that the student was very bright, talked a lot, was filled with ideas on how Indians were supposed to be, tribal sovereignty, the typical college discourse on Native issues. "But he has never really spent time around his own people, never been out to the grounds. That's why I called you." He explained how the student had gone home for long weekends with the other Native students and seemed well liked by the Natives on campus.

It was getting toward late afternoon, almost dusk, which was Jackson's favorite time of day. Well, besides morning, and night. And the moment right before morning with the first faint light when you are not really sure day is coming or if it is just wishful thinking. Jackson always thought of dusk as the moment between what was and that which was supposed to be, when things would come out. It was when he enjoyed sitting at the grounds, with friends and relations. It was a time to visit. As Jackson and his old friend found a small table on the patio, the Professor asked if Jackson wanted a cup of coffee or if it was too late. He knew the answer before he asked. It was never too late. Jackson always took coffee if offered.

"Yes, please. A small cup," Jackson said, pausing a moment, and added, "Make it two small cups."

The Professor didn't ask why not one large cup. He had been around Jackson too long to wonder about why he did what he did. There was almost always a reason. The Professor got two small cups of coffee and a sweet tea for himself, and sat down next to Jackson, placing both coffees in front of Jackson. Jackson said thank you and took one cup, removed the lid, and set it on the opposite side of the table. Then he took his lid off and held it in his hand, blowing on it for a moment before taking a sip. The Professor looked at Jackson, at the cup sitting there by itself, and back at Jackson but didn't say anything. That kind of thing was why he asked Jackson to come visit. They both just sat there and waited for the Professor's student.

The student, Steven, showed up shortly, sipping on his water bottle, and they made their introductions. After Steven shook Jackson's hand, he started to sit down across from Jackson, who told him to sit next to him, across from the Professor, the young man never noticing the extra cup. Steven pretty much started talking as soon as he sat down. He was really excited about some news he read about a sacred site issue on a reservation up north. He asked the Professor if he had ideas on how to build coalitions with their white allies, though he didn't seem to wait long for answers.

"What kinds of things are you studying at school?" Jackson finally asked. "What kind of work are you interested in?"

Steven responded that he was trying to learn whatever he could, maybe a project on sacred sites, as he felt Natives lived more fully in the spiritual world than the Western world, whose allegiance to materialism created a disconnect between the physical and spiritual. He talked about all the sacred sites out west or up north that needed protecting.

Jackson just listened, thinking this is a strange conversation to be having, considering my last few months. Finally, Steven seemed to run out of words or maybe he was just nervous meeting the Professor and an "elder," though Jackson didn't think of himself as such. Steven asked Jackson what he thought.

"Well," Jackson said, "I understand others' concern about the social and religious dissonance you mention. But sometimes, you have to move past simply repeating others' discourse on colonialism or on our people's epistemology. There are many modalities. Sometimes you must just base your understanding on actual participation. Sometimes you have to just dance."

Steven was a bit surprised, and a bit embarrassed at being surprised, to hear Jackson using those terms, so he just nodded and to his credit sat quietly. After a bit, Jackson asked him who his people were. Steven said he didn't know them that well, but he was named after his great-grandfather. Jackson nodded and said that he knew of him.

"If you really want to know, to understand," Jackson continued, "next week we are having a work party for our dances. If you want to come help, you can meet some of your relations, not sure any are real close, but relations nonetheless. Bring work gloves and boots. Chief said we need enough wood for the first few dances, and we should get it now. Your help would be appreciated."

Steven was not expecting that, but he seemed excited and agreed. He apologized but had to leave, he had to let his dog out and meet some others to study for a test. They all shook hands, and Steven went on his way.

"I should be on my way, too," Jackson said.

"What you think of the young man?" the Professor asked Jackson.

Jackson thought for a moment and said, "Well, if he shows up, that will be nice. If he is a worker, that will be good, and if he continues showing up, that will be helpful. If not, well . . ."

The Professor nodded and watched as Jackson stood up, took the cup of coffee sitting across from him, and went over to a tree at the edge of the patio, knelt down, paused, and carefully poured the coffee out. When Jackson came back over to the Professor, he told his friend thank you, he enjoyed visiting and having a chance to meet his student, but that he had best be heading home.

As he was turning to leave, Jackson stopped and said, "He certainly is interested in Indian things, seems committed to Indian causes. It's nice to see young people caring." Then Jackson asked, "Do you think he noticed the other coffee cup?"

"*Buh*, I don't think so!" the Professor said.

"Me either. Maybe he will in time."

The Professor didn't think Jackson was going to continue, so he told Jackson, "Well, I was wondering about it. Maybe you can tell me about it sometime. And say hi to Mary for me."

"*Huhn,*" Jackson laughed, "I will. And if someday I understand, I will try to tell you about it."

They shook hands, and Jackson headed to his truck. He thought to himself it was good to see his friend, good to meet the young man. It was good to get out. Maybe the young man would be okay, if he was willing to learn. He wondered what his friend the Old Man would have thought had he been there. As he drove out of town, Jackson felt a voice telling him, "Perhaps if you resolved your allegiance to materialism, you wouldn't be so disconnected from the spiritual world."

As he retraced his drive, Jackson rolled his eyes and said, "*Henju!* Who knew Spirits could be so sarcastic?"

Jackson Speaks for His Niece

It was early April, a beautiful Sunday afternoon in Euchee Country. The churches' onion dinners had everyone out visiting on Saturdays. The ceremonial people would be starting their ball games soon, if not already. Throwing the ball up, Indian football at Polecat, stickball at most of the others. That would start the stomp-dance season. But for now, Sunday afternoons were mostly still free, at least if you weren't much of a church person.

Jackson spent his morning doing some yard work. Then maybe a nice lunch for him and the wife. Nothing too heavy, as they were still feeling the salt meat from the day before. Jackson had laughed looking at his knuckles, thinking they were a bit fatter from all the salt. Afterward, he spent some time working on his truck. More like looking at it, and then sitting in it. Jackson called it working, one had to think about a thing before one did it. Now it was getting toward late afternoon, and with the warmth quickly fading, he started a fire, figured it was good practice using the flint. Not that he really needed practice after all these years. He enjoyed the fire, but the act of holding the rocks and punk, talking to them, getting the fireplace ready, felt comfortable, a continuity. He knew he should be doing something, sharpening the chainsaws, replacing the sparkplugs, tuning them. Work parties and dance season come up quick, always best to get things done early. He wished they would cut wood over the winter; they always talked about it, getting together and letting the wood season. They'd been saying that for years, he thought with a smile.

173

So Jackson was sitting in his truck with the door open, sharpening his knife and watching the fire, softly singing stomp-dance songs. Mary was in the house working on her quilts. She did beautiful work, mostly star quilts, sometimes wedding ring, sometimes special order for people. She had made quite a few funeral quilts, ones that people wanted for their casket when they were buried, the last covering as they were lowered into the ground. She was always honored for those, thinking of the lifetime of the people who ordered them. Usually, the orders were just for someone who wanted something special, old family fabric, an eagle star quilt, school colors for graduation, even for giveaways.

When Jackson's nephew Yaw-ah (Big Tree) showed up, that's where they were, an old married couple comfortably each doing their separate things. Yaw-ah was really his sister's grandson, but he called her Mom, most of the time, because she had raised Yaw-ah and his sister. That day he rang the doorbell, waited a minute, then knocked. When not even the dog came to the door, he grabbed the handle, opened the door, calling out as he went in, "Uncle? Auntie?" He spent so much time there growing up he usually just went in. Today, though, he was more formal. It felt strange, but his mom sent him over, so he tried to act proper, official business like. When Yaw-ah didn't see anyone in the living room, he figured Auntie was in her sewing room, at the end of the hallway just past the bathroom. Same layout as his mom's place, just different stuff in the rooms. He called out as he went back so as not to startle her, looking at the photos hanging on the walls as he went. He saw some of his mom when she was young, of him and his sister. There were some old black-and-whites, not sure who they were, maybe taken in the 1920s or even earlier. Some from the 1940s, maybe World War II, from the look of the uniforms and women's hair. There was one of Uncle Jackson in his army uniform, a small Polaroid, of Jackson in his fatigues, of him and his army buddies, obviously from when he was overseas. Yaw-ah always liked that photo. Uncle looked so, not sure what, maybe intense? Competent? An easy professionalism. A warrior. Not someone to be fucked with.

Those pictures, so many of them. Some old black-and-whites of people he didn't know. Maybe his great-grandparents, great-great-grandparents, faded with those almost bowl haircuts, in wool coats with wife and children, so formal looking. Other faded Polaroids from the 1950s and '60s. Faded color pictures of women lining up for Ribbon Dance at Green Corn, some looking serious, others laughing. School pictures, so many school pictures. He saw some of his, wondering why his mom dressed him like that, but he laughed, it was probably all his mom could do just to get him dressed and off to school. He paused, as he often did, to look at one of his dad in his army uniform, next to one of his dad in his football uniform doing the Heisman pose. Others he recognized as taken at funerals, all the cousins or aunts and uncles gathered up. Some people he recognized, others he had no clue about. So much history, silently staring at him as he paused to look, walking down the hallway. So often he just walked past them. Then he was at Auntie's sewing room as she was putting fabric away, getting up to hug him.

"*F'asahn!* Yaw-ah," she greeted.

He greeted her back and hugged her. Mary, always his favorite auntie. She knew more Euchee than these young ones, even though she was from up north.

"*Sahngala? Wigah nehfajehn?*" Wanting to know how he was, where he had been, where he was going, how his mom was? They exchanged pleasantries as she guided him back down the hall to the kitchen. Telling him to sit as she got him coffee and set it in front of him. Not even bothering to ask if he wanted it. Asking him if he was hungry. He responded, no, that he ate at his mom's before he came over.

She said, "Well, before you leave, you'll have some room for some cobbler."

"*Huhn,*" he agreed. Aunt Mary's cobbler was worth the visit.

After they'd visited for a bit, Aunt Mary simply said, "Uncle's out back. Might as well take the old man some coffee, too," as she filled another cup and gave it to her nephew.

With that, he picked up the cups, and with Auntie holding the door open, he went to find his uncle. He found Uncle with his truck, the hood up, looking at the alternator, maybe adjusting the wires. Jackson heard his nephew coming out the back door, wiped his hands with the red rag hanging from his back pocket, and waited for his nephew. Jackson took the offered coffee, and once Yaw-ah had a free hand, they shook hands and greeted each other. Jackson nodded his head toward the fireplace and the chairs, and as they sat down, they exchanged the usual small talk. About Nephew's mom, what Jackson had been doing, Aunt Mary's quilts, getting ready for the grounds, which of the Creek grounds didn't look like they would dance this year, or if one that had been down might start up again. Finally, as Jackson knew he would, Nephew got around to talking about why he came to visit.

"My mom wanted me to ask you for a favor," Yaw-ah said as he stood up.

Jackson sat waiting.

"You know my sister, she's about to graduate high school this May."

"*Huhn*," Jackson answered. "I know her. Heck of a ballplayer. We went and watched some of her games this year."

"Yup. She got some offers to play ball. Not any big-time schools, but still D-1. Anyway, she decided on her school and she's going to sign her letter in two weeks. Mom wants to have a dinner for her when she does." Then Yaw-ah paused.

Jackson said that would be good and waited. He knew his sister wouldn't have sent his nephew over just to invite him and Mary to the dinner. A phone call, or even texts, would've done fine for that. Yaw-ah reached into his jean jacket pocket and pulled out a white handkerchief, its four corners neatly tied at the top, appearing to hold a little bundle inside. Holding it in his left hand, Yaw-ah carefully pulled the knots loose. Inside was Days O Work plug tobacco. Jackson's nephew looked at the tobacco, absently touching it as he started speaking to Uncle Jackson.

"Mom wanted to send sister off to school, this signing, in a good way. She has already taken care of the food. Yesterday she asked Aunt Mary to cook."

Jackson nodded at that. Mary was a good cook, and knew what to make, and dependable. He was surprised she had managed not to say anything about it, as she usually shared that kind of thing. Or maybe his sister had asked her not to, he thought with a shrug. Yaw-ah continued, as he held the tobacco, rubbing it as if he was talking to it as much as to Jackson.

"So, anyway, Mom sent me to ask if you would talk for her at the dinner. Mom wanted to give you this tobacco, to ask if you would do this." With that, he handed Jackson the plug, and then the handkerchief.

Jackson stood up, took the offering, and shook his nephew's hand. Then, looking at the tobacco for a moment, Jackson put it back in the white handkerchief, folding it up, and said, "*Huhn*. I would be honored to speak. *Sahnle gaya dzoda.*" Then put the tobacco in his pocket.

Agreeing to help, he thought of his great-niece's dad, his sister's oldest boy, his nephew Sonny. Jackson asked Yaw-ah if anyone had really told him about his and his sister's dad? Yaw-ah said only bits, no one really said too much. So Jackson said, "Sit down. I'll tell you some." They sat, and Jackson began talking.

Sonny had been one of the best athletes in Oklahoma during high school, a wide receiver. He'd signed a D-1 scholarship for a big school.

Jackson couldn't remember which one, the Oklahoma schools had recruited him, but he wanted to go out of state, maybe Wisconsin or in Michigan, somewhere up north. He had also done a lot of rodeos when he was young, roping mostly, speed and skill. The summer after he graduated, he spent time rodeoing, working out, and going to dances. As the summer went by and time got closer for him to report to college, he became less sure what he wanted. His dad had been in the service, infantry, like Jackson and their grandfather. And other relations. He grew up listening to them talk about the service, seeing the old men under the arbors, raising the flag on Green Corn Day. Seeing them honored on Veterans Day, some marching in the parades. Finally, one day shortly after Green Corn, he went and told his mom he had enlisted and would leave in a month, about the time he should have been going off to college and football.

His mom started crying. She was so excited to see him playing ball on Saturdays, maybe even on television, to see him get an education. She was proud of her relations who had served, but she also knew there was a price some of them paid, even if most of them came back in one piece. What was done was done, though, so she told her boy how proud she was of him. Then she quickly got to arranging a dinner for him before he left for boot camp. Jackson told Yaw-ah he spoke for his dad at that dinner, too, speaking about the service and some of what he had been told as a warrior going off to the army.

The service must have agreed with him, because he spent the next dozen years in the service. And he, like so many Natives who joined, made it through to the special forces. He said it was mostly pretty boring, but he did two tours in Afghanistan. It was while he was on leave, "visiting" one of the local girls, that Yaw-ah came to be. And then a couple years later, the same girl had his daughter who was soon to graduate. He'd met the baby mom at a pow-wow in Tulsa. His daughter's birth was one of the reasons he got out of the service. The mom didn't really want to be a mom. Too much fun running the pow-wow circuit and partying. Sonny's mom had already been the main caretaker of Yaw-ah, and now with a daughter, he decided it was time to be a full-time dad. He had too many commitments, too much at risk to stay in. He got out of the service, came home, moved in with his mom, and started raising his son and baby daughter. He took some odd jobs, construction, occasionally with the tribe, and again made a little rodeo money. But what he started making real money at was his art.

When he was young, he was fascinated with old arrowheads. He began playing with, learning how to make flint arrowheads. At first, they were rough, even ugly. Over time, he got good at it, very good. He kept it up in the service, kept him busy. By the time he was thirty, his flint knives were things of beauty. Dark flint rock that he gathered when he visited his Cherokee friend by Tahlequah. Using deer horn for the handles with hand-tanned hides wrapped around the handles. He got the hides from a friend who lived on a reservation up north. People were always surprised at the stunningly sharp blades, how the handle fit perfectly in the hand. He always told people, with a laugh, that after a dozen years in the service, he knew what a weapon should feel like.

His pow-wow friends begged him for his knives and sheaths for their dance outfits. Collectors were beginning to notice his work, too. He would charge $100 to $150 for pow-wowers, maybe three times that to the white collectors. He loved working on the knives, he could almost feel the Old People, the Ancestors whose lives had depended on flint. The amount of time and energy it took to fashion a simple knife. How with that same flint his uncles would start the fire at the hill. Even the handle, deer, his clan, binding part of himself to the work.

That weekend, fifteen years earlier, Sonny had finished a matched set of knives and a spear. He got some bois d'arc from a Kickapoo friend that his friend used to make traditional bows. He was proud of how the three pieces came out, clean, sharp, perfectly balanced. His friend needed a knife for his dance outfit, so he had that one sold. The other knife and the spear a collector wanted. Sonny told him a price of $2,500, which included a cedar storage box; the collector agreed but wanted to see them first. There was a pow-wow and art show by Shawnee in a week, and the collector was coming in to attend. Sonny decided he could deliver all three that weekend.

Besides making some money, he felt the itch to get out and about. He didn't run around and drink like he used to. He behaved himself mostly, a good stay-at-home dad. His mom was sharing so much of the work. The children's mom may have seen the kids occasionally during the year, in passing, but no more than that. Still, he occasionally got the urge. Besides, he knew a few girls in the Shawnee area that would be happy to see him. On Thursday afternoon, he left his two kids with his mom, who suspected it was more than a sales trip, picked up his cousin, and headed out. It took about an hour and a half to get to a mutual friend's house in Shawnee.

Their friend was Shawnee and lived in one of those three-bedroom Indian homes. Sonny wondered if every Indian home everywhere, at least in Oklahoma, was built by the same crew. Small kitchen off a small dining area, a door to the garage or carport, which may have been closed in for more cold, unheated living space. The living room in front of the dining area with a wall separating the kitchen, and a hallway leading down to the bedrooms and bathroom. And, of course, a cheap dream-catcher hanging on the wall somewhere. Sonny and his cousin visited them for a while, but they all had to work in the morning, and they made it an early evening.

The next morning, they got up, said their thanks, and headed over to the pow-wow grounds. Sonny's friend who wanted the knife had a family camp, and they went to find it. They found his friend's family sitting around their camp visiting and getting things organized for the evening's grand entry. Sonny showed his friend the knife, who loved it, as did everyone else in camp. He kept thanking Sonny for bringing it to him. After drinking coffee and visiting in camp, catching up on other friends, and sharing service stories with his friend's dad and uncle, they decided to look at the vendors and, he said laughingly, to find his "great white benefactor." He told them how excited he was to sell the spear to the collector. His friend's family tried to convince him that the spear set belonged in the arena. Sonny replied, "Maybe it does, but the $2,500 belongs in my pocket!" They all laughingly agreed and made plans to meet up later, telling Sonny they'd put a blanket on the bleachers by their chairs for him and his cousin to save them a spot.

For the next hour or two, they wandered around the vendors area, stopping occasionally to talk to friends. Sonny had made arrangements to meet the collector around 1:00 P.M., thus they took their time. Sonny was excited, this would be the biggest sale he'd made, and hoped it would spark more high-end art collectors. The collector was from Pittsburg, in his midfifties, and was originally interested in historic weapons—samurai swords, medieval armor, and such. But he collected Native art and had met Sonny at a mutual friend's booth at the Santa Fe Art Market two years before. As Sonny and the collector visited, they discovered a mutual love for weapons and knives, the collector telling Sonny that if he ever got to making any really nice pieces, to let him know. So here they were, meeting in Shawnee.

When the collector saw Sonny's work, he was ecstatic, asking Sonny all about how he made it. So excited, running his finger gently over the razor-sharp flint edges. The collector paid Sonny by check, even adding an additional $100 for "gas money" for his bringing it to Shawnee. Sonny wasn't worried about the check bouncing, having seen the collector drop $12,000 for two turquoise and gold bolos in Santa Fe. And he had flown in his private jet from Pittsburg. It struck Sonny how these art collectors wanted so much to be part of Indian culture, wearing all the clothes and jewelry. And how he would love to have the money and life of the rich art collectors. But he put those thoughts to the side and figured he better get to the bank to deposit the check. Luckily, his bank had a branch in Shawnee. Sonny and his cousin left the pow-wow ground, jumped in his truck, and went off to the bank. He deposited the check, keeping the $150 from his friend plus another $50 cash for "play money."

By that time, it was mid- to late afternoon, and they were getting hungry, thinking of where to eat. His cousin said, "We can't come all the way to Shawnee and not eat at Hamburger King." So that's where they went. After finishing, it was time to head back to the pow-wow and their friend's camp. Everyone was dressing for grand entry, laughing, and visiting. Trying to keep half an eye on the kids running around. They told Sonny they had saved a spot for the two of them. His friend's mom and aunts were serving everyone supper. Despite having eaten just before, they didn't want to be disrespectful, and the fry bread and hominy smelled so good. Then it was grand entry time.

That evening, between Sonny being known for football, rodeo, a veteran, and a good-looking man, there was a study stream of visitors, mostly young women, to where Sonny sat. Sonny wasn't a pow-wower, but he could dance, and got pulled out for more than several dances that evening. One girl in particular seemed to catch his eye, she must have been in her late twenties, a jingle dancer who had been a tribal princess a few years earlier. Very beautiful, athletic looking, long black hair in tight braids. She and her girlfriend came over to visit Sonny's friend's sister, at least twice that evening, managing to speak more with Sonny than the sister, eventually asking Sonny if he was going to the '49 (the "after the pow-wow" pow-wow) that night. He hadn't been to a '49 in quite a while, but it seemed like now might be a good time to go again. In the meantime, he continued watching and visiting till the dancing ended around midnight.

After that, what happened becomes a little vague, maybe alcohol fog, or maybe just because it was dark, late, and no one was wanting to talk. But Sonny and his cousin went to the '49. However, sometime around

2:30 A.M. they found Sonny's truck overturned on the old highway, an empty twelve pack of beer in the cab, with him thrown from the vehicle. The jingle dancer was still buckled in the truck, which the highway patrol said saved her life. Sonny was not so lucky, probably dying on impact. Sonny's cousin wasn't in the truck, having stayed at the '49 trying to snag.

Jackson told Yaw-ah that he had fixed medicine for his dad's funeral. That was a hard time for Jackson's sister. Jackson continued, "Your mom, your *golaha* really, she took it hard. You were too young to understand most of that, not sure what you remembered. But I thought maybe you might want to know, now that you and your sister are both grown up."

Yaw-ah nodded. He had only heard parts of the story Jackson told, mostly about his dad's service. And that something had happened. But he was glad to have Uncle Jackson tell him now. They stayed there, both quiet for a time, thinking about what happened. Both wondering how different it might have been if Sonny were still around. So much talent, so much goodness stolen from them.

Finally, Jackson said, "I hope that you know what a good man your dad was. But one mistake can change everything. And we Indians suffer too many one mistakes. You remember that, Nephew." Yaw-ah nodded again. Jackson paused, then went on, "Tell my sister I will be there. I will be honored to speak for Niece. *Sahnle gaya dzoda.*" With that, they walked up to the house, and Nephew said good-bye to Aunt Mary, who made him take a piece of cobbler for later.

The Euchee Parting

Nowadays, at our grounds, one hears mostly the same songs as at other non-Euchee grounds. But when I was younger, Kagowe, one of the old men at the stomp ground, would occasionally sing Euchee songs. Kagowe knew old songs, ones that were of our Euchee people. Distinct, Euchee. Old songs. Some of them with words in them. Our friends, the Creeks, seem to have a lot of songs with Muscogee words or stories. But the old Euchee said our language was difficult to sound right when put into stomp-dance songs. Kagowe tried to teach me one with Euchee words, that told a story. But I didn't catch it that night, and never had the chance to hear it again. The poem that follows is based on that song, though I don't remember the actual Euchee lyrics. I used to think this story was from during removal, the Trail of Tears, in the 1830s. However, the older I get the more I think this comes from much further back in our past. This is my own attempt to tell what Kagowe tried to teach me.

Gahsthale aheiha,
  (When they were all here,)
Eucheeha hînû hok'aju ahênûe jehnfa.
  (All the Euchee were all together.)

Go-hane hinû hôgwanejehn,
  (The old men said,)
f'âfa-ji.
  (they were going West.)
f'anfa-âji hi-suh-lale.
  (We were all going West.)

Neh-yahle diwi,
  (Don't look back,)
Neh-yahle diwi.
  (Don't look back.)

We stopped at a good place,
This was a clean place.
We stopped for the night.

The young boys gathered wood,
The old men lit the fire.

Our relations said,
Neh-chi s'ah sahnle.
  (This is a good place.)
Other relations said,
F'âfa nôfeguhn.
  (To the west we must go.)

The Old People gathered,
The Old People talked, each in turn.
The Old People listened, then they decided.

Abe f'âchi, goshti.
  (Tonight, we dance.)
Abe f'âchi, yagwane.
  (Tonight, we sing.)

Agahe, Dzonuh Ondzehê ubale.
  (Tomorrow, when Mother Sun rises.)
Aga dâda agæ, hôfena.
  (When first light comes, they will go.)

Aga dâda agæ, âdze s'æha.
   (When first light comes, we will stay.)
And that is what they did.

Neh-yahle diwi,
Neh-yahle diwi,

Nôde âdze yagwajehn,
   (Then we sang.)
Nôda âdze goshtijehn.
   (Then we danced.)

When the Sun rose,
when her light came,
we closed the door.

Goshti dehe-jehn,
   (After the dance,)
Nuȟdzo dzo-gala f'âfa hôfa-jehn.
   (our relations went west.)
Goshti dehe-jehn,
   (After the dance,)
Nuȟdzo gene nuhjehn.
   (We stayed behind.)

Those who went are gone.
Lehinû nû-dineh-jehn.
   (I have not seen them.)

Neh-yahle diwi.
Neh-yahle diwi.

That is what they say.

❧
Rabbit and the Last
Old Woman

"Rabbit and the Last Old Woman" is a new creation, like some of the others before it, patterned on stories heard from elderly Euchee women. It was originally included in an article for the UCLA Law School's Indigenous Peoples' Journal of Law, Culture, and Resistance *7, no. 1, "Foundations of Tribal Society: Art, Dreams, and the Last Old Woman." It began an exploration of what might happen to us, and our characters, when we cease telling our stories. It is meant to illustrate how these simple stories tell much about our tribal society and how we can look for markers of a healthy vibrant Indigenous society. When one thinks of all the things that have impacted poor Rabbit, I think he faces two possible worlds, the one that you already read about, which is disappearing, or at least hiding. And the other world that may yet be created by the dedication of our language learners, storytellers, legal advocates, international representatives, and people who care and learn.*

William Cahwee, now deceased for some years, was one of my elder language speakers. He loved his Euchee language and was a deep thinker of the nature of our language. He explained that "dilehuhn" is an indefinite future particle attached to the end of contemplated actions. William would explain that if you're stating an action that is to occur in the future, you use this particle. One never knows, William would say, what the future might hold. Until it occurs, it is unknown what will be. For instance, I was taught by my old chief and other elders that when calling out leaders for the next dance at the

stomp grounds one would say in Euchee: "Another leader has agreed
to lead (maybe)." Because until he comes out, one does not know if it
will be. Will he come out to lead or won't he come out to lead? Once
that occurs, then we know. (Which is not an unheard-of occurrence;
it has happened to me in the past.) Understanding our future and
Shajwane's in this context, an alternative ending to "Rabbit and the
Last Old Woman" came to mind. In the end, perhaps Rabbit will
simply be a rabbit, or perhaps he climbs that hill and looks to the
future. Perhaps one has hope in what might occur. Which one
becomes true is not yet known. It may be up to you.

When it used to be that some of them were still here, they said
Rabbit was thinking he had not seen his friend Bear in a long
time. He decided the next day he would go to find him. It
seemed there were many friends he could not remember seeing. As he
began walking down the trail, he thought of the many times he had done
this before, past the briar patches, the fields. Things, though, seemed
to be changed, things were different, he thought. As he went over the
hill he looked around as he always did to see if any turkeys were there.
He had brought his sack just in case. But, again, as it had been for a
long time, there were no turkeys. He paused to listen, but he did not
hear even a faint gobble. With a slight shrug, he went on his way. No
turkeys, no laughter. No meal tonight, he laughed.

Finally, in the distance he saw Bear and called out to him: "My friend,
my friend, wait!" Bear seemed happy to see Rabbit and told him, "Sit
here by my fire, and we will visit." Rabbit was happy, but thought his
friend was not his usual big self. Rabbit had always been a bit jealous of
his friend, of his size and strength.

He asked Bear, "How are you? Is everything okay?"

Bear said, "You are the first one I have seen in a long time. I don't
know where everyone else has gone."

Rabbit wasn't sure what Bear meant, and asked, "Gone?? What do
you mean? Did you eat them?"

Bear looked at Rabbit and laughed, "I might have, my friend . . ."

Rabbit looked alarmed and took a step back.

Bear continued, "No, I didn't eat them. Maybe they are not all gone,
but when I do see them and talk to them, they run away, or they just
look at me, like my dog. I don't think they understand. It is very strange.
It's like they are not really here."

Rabbit with coffee. Illustration by Adam Youngbear.

Then Bear was quiet. They sat there for a long time not saying anything, watching the fire. It was getting late, so Rabbit told Bear he had better return home. So they shook hands, and Rabbit got up to leave.

As Rabbit turned, Bear said, "Rabbit, we have been friends, visiting, dancing, sharing meals, for a very long time. I can't remember a time not being your friend. We have many stories. But I think this may be our last. Thank you. You are a good friend, my brother. Always remember if this comes to be, always be yourself."

And with that, Rabbit left and Bear was gone.

Rabbit thought about what Bear said as he walked home. He put his hand on his stomach, remembering, quietly returning home. The woods seemed smaller as he walked, the fields overgrown. Rabbit felt lonely and decided he would stop by the Old Woman's house on the way. Besides, she always had something to eat. Maybe she would know what Bear was talking about. The Old Women knew many things, she might know why things were this way.

As he walked up to her home, he yelled out, "Golaha! Are you home?" He heard a voice, "*Huhn.* Come in."

There she was, sitting at her table. She asked him if he was hungry, which he was. After she fed him, she told him she was happy to see him. She, too, had not had any visitors in a long time. Rabbit noticed she looked very old. And frail. Even for her. He mentioned this.

She looked at him, "An old woman gets lonely by herself."

"I'm surprised, you were always the best storyteller," Rabbit said.

"And you always gave me so many to tell!" she laughed.

Rabbit was not sure that was a good thing, but she was a good cook, so he didn't mind too much and told her, "It seems odd you have no visitors."

She continued, "Yes, I know. I have so many stories to tell but no one to tell them to." Rabbit finished his soup and was about to leave when she turned to him, "I am an old woman. I may not be here the next time. None of us know what will come. None of us thought this would happen, but it has. I have no one to tell about you or the others. You have already lost many of your friends. We don't have a word for this, so I will use theirs—I am sorry. I tried. Thank you, Shajwane, my little friend, for all you have done."

With that, she spit on the floor, and Rabbit turned and left. When he looked back, the Old Woman was gone. Rabbit began walking, wondering what she had meant. It seemed very strange and a little scary. He thought, "I just don't know," and began hopping home.

That is what they will say.

Alternate Ending—Rabbit and the Last Old Woman

With that, the Old Woman spit on the floor, and Rabbit turned and left. When he looked back, all he could see was mist where her house should be. Rabbit felt a chill and began hurrying on his way. He wondered about what she had told him, it seemed strange, and worrisome. He thought of his friends, Bear, Crane, the Old Woman, the Spirits. He carried their words along the path he was taking, toward his home. He was not sure what it all meant and felt a sadness, but a warmth, too, thinking of what had been on the long road behind.

As he went, he saw a hill ahead. One which he always went past but never up. Today, though, this late afternoon, thinking of his friends and relations, he decided he would climb the hill. Once begun, it did not take long for Shajwane to reach the summit. As he stood looking from the top, he realized how far he could see. So much that lay ahead. Rabbit stood for a time, looking and thinking. He thought of his wife and children, and with some luck, grandchildren yet to come. All these thoughts settled upon him like smoke from the fireplace on a warm, still summer night. Finally, it was dusk. Dusk, that gray moment between what was in the light of day and what might be in the dark of night. When the worlds are merged and things might yet be possible. When stories become real. It was time for Shajwane to go.

As he moved forward, Rabbit felt happiness, and a need to dance.

"*Hoy-yoy, hoy-yoy.*" Stomp, stomp.

"*Hey-yay, hey-yay.*" Stomp, stomp.

Shajwane weshti dile-huhn.[1]

Notes

Introduction

1. In May 2022, the Department of the Interior released its Federal Indian Boarding School Initiative Investigative Report, which recognized the intentional destruction of Native languages as part of the effort to destroy tribal culture and thus ease the process of dispossessing Indians of their lands.

2. *United Nations Declaration on the Rights of Indigenous Peoples* (A/RES/ 61/295), Article 31.1: "Indigenous peoples have the right to maintain, control, protect, and develop their cultural heritage, traditional knowledge, and traditional cultural expressions, as well as the manifestations of their sciences, technologies, and cultures, including human and genetic resources, seeds, medicines, knowledge of the properties of fauna and flora, oral traditions, literatures, designs, sports and traditional games, and visual and performing arts. They also have the right to maintain, control, protect, and develop their intellectual property over such cultural heritage, traditional knowledge, and traditional cultural expressions. 2. In conjunction with indigenous peoples, States shall take effective measures to recognize and protect the exercise of these rights."

3. Muscogee (Creek) Nation, TR-16-149, *Muscogee Declaration on the Rights of Indigenous Peoples*, Article 31: *Hiyomakat pum ayetv pum wihokat vcacvket omet sahkopanetvt okot omes.* See English translation at https://creekdistrictcourt.com /wp-content/uploads/2019/08/Mvskoke-DRIP-031619.pdf.

4. I wish to express my deep appreciation to Yoney Spencer and Tamara Wilson, both of the Euchee Language Learning Center (and Polecat Ceremonial Stomp Grounds) for their assistance with the Euchee wording herein. However, any "misspellings," incorrect syntax, or other errors with the Euchee wording are mine.

Part 1

1. How one measures fluency can be a point of dispute in language revitalization efforts. However, for us it was clear: those who could speak without dropping into English were fluent, the rest of us were not. The difference was quite dramatic.

2. Pub.L. 101–601; 25 U.S.C. 3001–3013;104 Stat. 3048–3058.

3. These efforts, though not formal, continued in the early 2000s. In speaking with current students, they continue to raise the issue, expressing reluctance to visit the Peabody Museum because it houses ancestral remains.

4. Cara J. Chang, "Harvard Holds Human Remains of 19 Likely Enslaved Individuals, Thousands of Native Americans, Draft Report Says," *Harvard Crimson*, June 1, 2022.

5. G. H. Bigler, "Foundations of Tribal Society: Art, Dreams, and the Last Old Woman," *The Indigenous Peoples' Journal of Law, Culture & Resistance* 7, no. 1 (2022). Retrieved from https://escholarship.org/uc/item/3rq6f519.

Part 2

1. Patrick Wolfe, "Settler Colonialism and the Elimination of the Native," *Journal of Genocide Research* 8, no. 4 (2006): 387–409. DOI: 10.1080/146 23520601056240.

2. See *American Indian Law Review* 43, no. 1 (2018), https://digitalcommons .law.ou.edu/ailr/v0143/iss1/2.

3. "They used to be here" is the traditional opening form of Euchee storytelling.

4. Rabbit had probably happened upon such works as Jodi A. Byrd and Michael Rothberg, "Between Subalternity and Indigeneity," *International Journal of Postcolonial Studies* 13, no. 1 (2011): 1–12, DOI: 10.1080/1369801X .2011.545574, p. 3), in which the authors state that "the development of an indigenous critical theory interrogating the concept of indigeneity may seem far from the interrogation of subalternity by postcolonial thinkers."

5. See "Shajwane and Gojithlah (Rabbit and Monster)" in this part.

6. In this context, "getting doctored" means to see a traditional Indian doctor, what some others might call a medicine man. Among our people, Indian doctors would treat a great many maladies, using a great number of plants combined with medicine songs. It was both physical and spiritual healing.

7. Bear, of course, was already doing bear things. Like when a young woman questioned my elderly fluent Euchee-speaking mother as to whether she preferred being called Native American, Indigenous, or First Nations. After the woman left, my mother remarked to us, "I grew up as an Indian, but really I am just Euchee." See Gregory H. Bigler, "Traditional Jurisprudence and Protection of Our Society: A Jurisgenerative Tail," *American Indian Law Review* 43, no. 1 (2018). Bear simply needed to do more bear things.

8. "[T]he experience of pleasure, joy, or self-satisfaction that comes from learning of or witnessing the troubles, failures, or humiliation of another. Schadenfreude is a complex emotion, where rather than feeling sympathy

toward someone's misfortune, schadenfreude evokes joyful feelings that take pleasure from watching someone fail." Wikipedia.

9. Ida Riley (Clinton), who was a remarkable storyteller and whose father, George Clinton, was the source of many stories in Gunter Wagner's 1936 work *Yuchi Tales*, used this translanguage constructive modality in our version of "Shajwane and Gojithlah (Rabbit and Monster)," supra. While Ida told the story in Euchee, she has Rabbit say in English "I don't know" to show he can speak English to impress the girls. In this case, Rabbit is using German at the same time he is extolling returning to our own "true selves."

Part 3

1. Euchee for ten.
2. "I sure did hear something."
3. One of the traditional Euchee hymns repeats a refrain, "Everyone come along, do not fall behind," inserting in each subsequent verse "Christians come along," "Brothers . . . ," "Sisters . . . ," "Friends . . . ." While the hymn can be understood as being about following the Christian path, it can also be understood as telling the story of our removal from Georgia on the Trail of Tears in the 1830s and all the other journeys of our people.

Part 4

No notes.

Part 5

1. "It may be that Rabbit danced."

www.ingramcontent.com/pod-product-compliance
Lightning Source LLC
Chambersburg PA
CBHW031502161224
19094CB00002B/92